Running Records

Authentic Instruction in Early Childhood Education

Mary Shea

D1367005

Routledge
Taylor & Francis Group

NEW YORK AND LONDON

First published 2012
by Routledge
711 Third Avenue, New York, NY 10017

Simultaneously published in the UK
by Routledge
2 Park Square, Milton Park, Abingdon, Oxon OX14 4RN

Routledge is an imprint of the Taylor & Francis Group, an informa business

Library of Congress Cataloging in Publication Data
Shea, Mary (Mary E.)
   Running records : authentic instruction in early childhood education /
Mary Shea.
      p. cm.
   Includes bibliographical references and index.
   1. Reading (Elementary)—Ability testing. 2. Individualized instruction.
I. Title.
   LB1573.S471 2012
   372.4—dc23   2011044991

ISBN 13: 978-0-415-50379-2 (hbk)
ISBN 13: 978-0-415-50381-5 (pbk)
ISBN 13: 978-0-203-12040-8 (ebk)

Typeset in Minion Pro
by Cenveo Publisher Services

Please visit the companion website at

www.routledge.com/cw/shea

SFI
Certified Sourcing
www.sfiprogram.org
SFI-00453

Printed and bound in the United States of America
by Edwards Brothers, Inc.

This book is dedicated in loving memory to Patrick, Patricia, and Bernice.

CONTENTS

PREFACE

THIS BOOK

The increased diversity in classrooms has frustrated teachers who realize that old methods no longer work (Dodge, 2005). Some never did. They've witnessed the ineffectiveness of scripted programs, standardized curriculum, and high stakes tests. The professional community has begun to recognize that learners' lack of responsiveness to well-delivered, standardized instruction is not always related to internal problems. Appropriate and timely adjustments in instruction can ameliorate a lack of achievement. But, that instruction must be targeted. It must be based on data gathered from ongoing assessment, address immediate learning needs, and pave the way for further progress.

Although managing a classroom (i.e. content, methods, assignments, and environment) in which differentiated instruction flourishes is difficult, it is doable (Tomlinson, 1995, 1999, 2000, 2004, 2008; Tomlinson & Strickland, 2005). This book does not expand on that topic which is fully addressed in other texts. Rather, it focuses on an assessment that can undergird implementation of the tenets of differentiation.

THEMES

This text describes the concept of *differentiated instruction* as the foundation for *responsive teaching*. (Both concepts are defined and explored in Chapter 1.) Such teaching assumes that all children learn when provided with the appropriate type and amount of quality instruction; it's the basis for the *Response to Intervention* (RTI) process

in the United States. In order to move toward instructional practices which are appropriately responsive to learners' strengths, needs,
and/or interests, teachers need to accurately and efficiently identify
these ever changing attributes on a day-to-day basis. This requires keen
observation and ongoing assessment of small behaviors and performances; running records (RRs) offer a venue for meeting those objectives.
RRs involve a multi-dimensional assessment that allows teachers to
gather observational and quantitative data on a reader's performance—
an assessment that's reliable, useful, and efficient. Guided by
RR data, teachers plan for differentiated instruction; they also differentiate *in-the-moment* as children respond to that instruction.

Across the wide assortment of assessments for measuring children's
current level of reading competence, there's not one that can compare
to running records with regard to the amount, variation, and accuracy
of data that can be gathered; a RR involves a child's authentic, integrated performance of multiple reading skills. And, a RR can be done
without all the trappings of published packages that include printed
copies of text segments, prepared questions, and other accoutrements.
This book demonstrates how teachers can use running records to
determine the appropriateness of *any* text for *any* reader. Teachers'
ability to use RRs spontaneously allows them to determine the
appropriateness of particular resources for individual children. These
RRs are more efficient and cost effective than packaged assessments.
Understanding all that a RR reveals and planning for responsive
instruction based on that knowledge are themes explored across
chapters that follow an introduction to the RR process.

Key Concept

Response to Intervention (RTI): an instructional model that
supports success for all students through prevention, need identification, and targeted adjustments by offering multiple levels
(tiers) of teaching interventions based on children's responsiveness to student-centered instruction and assessment.

ORGANIZATION

To avoid the cumbersome use of he/she in the narrative when
identifying a student or teacher, gender specific pronouns (e.g. she, he,
his, her) are used across the text. The use of varied pronouns also

recognizes that most classroom communities include members of both sexes.

Part I of this text provides a rationale for the use of running records as an authentic, multi-faceted assessment that can be used to inform differentiated teaching. Chapter 1 (Introduction) examines the concept of differentiated instruction and responsive teaching—a concept universally accepted as essential for effective teaching. This concept is the basis for the *Response to Intervention* (RTI) process in the United States—a process for ameliorating learning difficulties before they escalate and for assuring that alternative methods, environments, grouping, and/or materials have been tried before learners are identified for special services. A chapter on RTI can be found at the companion website www.routledge.com/cw/shea.

Chapter 2 defines the attributes of authentic assessment and builds a case for the ongoing use of such measures in the classroom. Assessments that have utility are also aligned with curricular goals and objectives; these curriculum-based measures (CBMs) are critically important for effectiveness in any responsive teaching cycle (Hintze, Christ, & Methe, 2006). Deno (1987) described CBMs as involving "direct observation and recording of a student's performance in the local curriculum as a basis for gathering information to make instructional decisions" (p. 41).

Suggestions for using running records as formative and summative CBMs are offered. Continuous assessment of the learner's performance provides information for adjusting instruction—for responsive teaching. Guiding students along the path while removing roadblocks in learning to read with comprehension leads to success that builds confidence, independence, and competence.

Part II of the text (Chapter 3) focuses on the steps for taking a full running record (oral reading *and* learner's self-initiated retelling) and efficiently documenting data gathered. Models are provided throughout the chapter for each part of the process as well as at the companion website. Chapter 3 details the process for taking the RR, including the use of marking codes, measuring word accuracy, fluency, and comprehension, and analyzing miscues. RRs can be used for ongoing assessment in the process of monitoring reading growth, identifying strengths and needs, and documenting progress. Efficient RR documentation is critically important for planning targeted, meaningful instruction for each learner.

Part III of the text (Chapters 4–6) guides the reader in digging deeper into data collected during the running record, assessing the reader's current level of word reading accuracy, fluency, and comprehension with a particular text. The interaction across these aspects of the reading act as well as other factors that impact a reader's success with particular texts (e.g. text level, quality, genre, and background knowledge on the content) is also examined.

Part IV of the text (Chapters 7–9) offers suggestions for applying the information gathered from running records to differentiate and fine tune instruction in word recognition, reading fluency, and comprehension, making it tailored to readers' needs. A separate chapter explores differentiating instruction in each area.

The conclusion suggests ways to put the pieces together, specifically how to organize the classroom for responsive, differentiated instruction and manage the flow of interactions. Change in this direction will be easier when everyone works together, understands the purpose and promise of such instruction, and persists when working through obstacles. The rewards for learners are too great to miss.

A website accompanies the book. Among other resources at the website, you'll find a video segment of a child reading aloud as well as the teacher's scoring on marking forms. Use these to practice the process step-by-step. When you're ready to take running records with your students, use the blank forms provided at the website.

In addition, you'll find a chapter on RTI at the companion website: www.routledge.com/cw/shea. Across the United States, school districts are implementing or are in the process of planning for implementation of protocols that outline multi-tiered instructional responses for struggling learners. These are intended to identify the source of any learning glitch, ameliorate it, and move the learner forward on a continuum of achievement. *Differentiated instruction,* a concept associated with effective instruction, is at the core of the RTI process. Running records can be used to assess learners' literacy progress at each tier of intervention; they also provide documentation of students' responsiveness to instruction at each RTI tier or in any classroom dedicated to responsive teaching.

KEY FEATURES

In this text, readers are provided with a detailed, research-based rationale for the use of running records. This includes information on differentiated instruction, responsive teaching, and the RTI process as noted.

Step-by-step, the RR process is described and models are provided. Readers comfortably learn how to take and implement RRs in their classroom—ones that don't rely on publishers' packaged materials.

Video and additional resources on the companion website support concepts presented throughout the text.

Each aspect of data collected from a RR is examined for what it reveals about the reader's current level of competence with that skill. Suggestions for instruction intended to ameliorate confusion, reinforce skills, and/or advance readers to the next goal are discussed in chapters focused on various aspects of the reading process (e.g. word recognition, fluency, comprehension).

At the beginning of chapters, readers will find an advance organizer or list of key terms that set a purpose for reading and/or a guide for monitoring one's comprehension. Prompts at the end of chapters stimulate personal reflection or group discussions in grade level or school wide meetings as well as staff development sessions.

As previously mentioned, www.routledge.com/cw/shea offers several additional resources related to the topics addressed in the text. Each is intended to enhance the reader's understanding of why, how, and when RRs can be used in the teaching process to create classrooms where differentiated instruction, responsive teaching, child-centered learning, and sensitivity to diversity characterize all interactions.

ACKNOWLEDGMENTS

My learning comes from interaction with others. Sometimes the contact is indirect and, at other times, it's very local. The authors of texts and research reports I've read continue to fuel my thinking. More directly, the children and teachers I work with continuously expand my repertoire of professional knowledge and skills. I remain a work in progress—grateful to my sources of learning and inspiration. Integrating multiple sources of available information always helps me discern the next best step for instruction at any level.

I wish to thank the teachers and children who contributed material to this text and the running record examples in the book and at the website. Their work on that assessment measure provides a model that brings the concepts and procedures to life. Each example helps us realize how much qualitative and quantitative data can be acquired in this comfortable interaction. I am grateful to Learning A-Z for permission to provide the script for *Monkey to the Top*. The child is reading from this text in the videos at the website.

I am grateful to the teachers who shared details related to how *Response to Intervention* (RTI) works in their district. RTI is a multi-tiered process for supporting students who are struggling learners; it has begun to be implemented across the United States. The information teachers shared on RTI at the local level was incorporated into the RTI chapter at the website. This makes clear how site specific the application of RTI models becomes while including common purposes and goals. Teachers' queries about the origins of RTI led to a search for concepts that traced the development of RTI thinking. This basis for

RTI is described in the Introduction with a discussion of *differentiated instruction* as a foundation for effective practice in any classroom.

I am always grateful for the support of friends and family; it makes whatever I do possible. From them I find encouragement when I get bogged down; I find respite when I need a break from the task at hand.

Thanks so much to Alex Masulis, Editor at Routledge/Taylor & Francis, for his input and suggestions related to this text. He was always responsive to big and small questions all along the way, easing my mind and directing me along the path to completion. Special thanks as well to Katie Raissian, Meesha Nehru, and Sue Cope for all their fine tuning in the form of editing this text. I appreciate all the behind the scenes people at Routledge/Taylor & Francis who take care of business aspects (i.e. permissions and contracts). I appreciate the artistic talent of those who work on the production part of the process. As if by magic, they transform my writing and all the ancillary pieces I prepare into a text!

I continue to recognize the completion of any effort as a collaborative event. Others contribute in large and small ways to whatever I accomplish. I feel fortunate for their presence and influence.

Part I
Rationale for Running Records
Meeting the Diverse Needs of Learners

1

INTRODUCTION—DIFFERENTIATING INSTRUCTION

Responsive Teaching Informed by Ongoing Assessment

Big Ideas

Problem with standardization
Inclusive teaching for achievement of learning goals
Differentiated instruction
Differentiating content, process, product, and environment
Assessment that supports instructional differentiation

STANDARDIZED INSTRUCTION WITH NONSTANDARD STUDENTS

Ohanian (1999) exposes the fallacy of working with a standard timetable in classrooms with gloriously nonstandard kids. Different experiences, background, interests, motivations, talents, cultural heritage, and other factors have shaped their uniqueness—their *nonstandardess*. She emphasizes that "one size [curriculum] fits few" in schools today (Ohanian, 1999).

Effective curriculum planning considers the identified and potential needs of all students, balancing excellence of content and equity in

3

delivery with assessment that continuously informs instruction for each learner. Such curriculum outlines a process for meeting state standards across diverse populations (Fahey, 2000). Programs that disregard diversity—favoring standardization in instruction, materials, and products—are least likely to ensure that all children learn. Sadly, many are left behind (Tomlinson, 2004) when teachers are required to implement programs in standardized ways rather than teach children.

Key Concepts

Standardized instruction: uniform, scripted lessons used to ensure that all teachers conform to an accepted mode and timeline for content presentation.

Nonstandard: unique; having individual qualities across a variety of spectrums.

INCLUSIVE TEACHING FOR UNIVERSAL LEARNING OF CURRICULUM

Tobin (2008) describes the *universal design* curriculum model as one that includes instructional differentiation (responsive teaching) at all levels. Such instruction must be tied to immediate, in-the-moment assessment to be effective. In the current classrooms of diversity, responsive teaching is essential for success. Most students are able to benefit from initial instruction that's learner-centered. But, some don't. In such cases, in-the-moment assessment is essential. It reveals differences in interests, background knowledge, or needs and expedites the recognition of any learning glitch; it informs instruction that ameliorates the situation (Shea, Murray, & Harlin, 2005).

When learning is interrupted, teachers act in *intelligently eclectic* ways (Smith, 1983); they carefully consider students' individual strengths and needs before selecting an intervention that provides a different route to the same learning outcomes. They use authentic assessment to observe learners in a full performance of target behaviors; data gathered help them decide what the learner has confused, which materials are appropriate, and/or the best approach for teaching this child. Good teachers efficiently implement planned and in-the-moment responsive teaching based on data gathered; they make content and/or skills accessible to learners who were previously nonresponsive (not learning). When their interests and needs are aligned with learning opportunities, students perceive curricular outcomes as achievable (Pettig, 2000).

Key Concepts

Inclusive teaching: instructional approach that includes a range of appropriate strategies, ensuring that all children have an opportunity to learn.

Universal design: an approach for designing units of study that considers the what (content), how (strategies), and why (affect) of learning in ways that consider individual learners' needs.

Differentiation: appropriately adjusting the content, process, product, and the environment in a learning event to enhance students' opportunities for success.

Responsive teaching: instruction that includes ongoing assessment and responds immediately, adjusting instruction to fit the learner's expressed needs, strengths, or interests.

Eclectic: selecting from appropriate options the instructional approaches and resources best suited for individual learners.

PROACTIVE DIFFERENTIATED INSTRUCTION: INCREASING ACHIEVEMENT FOR ALL

"Differentiation embodies the philosophy that all students can learn—in their own way and in their own time" (Dodge, 2005, p. 6). Differentiated instruction (responsive teaching) focuses on curricular outcomes, helping all children meet and exceed established standards (Tomlinson, 2000). But, it starts with the child—and the teacher—not the content (Dodge, 2005). Kusuma-Powell and Powell (2004) identify the knowledge and skills that teachers need to hone for successful differentiating.

1. Thorough understanding of students' strengths and needs. To establish appropriate objectives teachers must know the learner, specifically what he knows and can do at any time (Littky, 2004). This requires authentic, ongoing assessment *of* learning

(summative assessment) and *for* learning (formative assessment) (Stiggins, 2002; Shea et al., 2005)

2. Knowledge of the scope and depth of curricular content. Teachers need to set learning goals that are grounded in the curriculum; lessons are crafted in ways that engage students in meaningful, developmentally appropriate tasks (Tomlinson, 2008). Instruction follows careful analysis of assessment data gathered from classroom activities (Shea et al., 2005).

3. Knowledge of best instructional practices and expertise in using them (e.g. flexible grouping, student choice, wait time, effective feedback).

4. Skills in collaborative planning, assessment, and reflection.

At the center of any effectively differentiated classroom—one where the teacher teaches responsively—you'll find sound theoretical, research-based practices implemented by a teacher with a broad repertoire of instructional skills and professional knowledge (Silver, Strong, & Perini, 2001; Tobin, 2008). These teachers assess each child's readiness (background knowledge on the topic and specific skills), talents, interests, motivation, and other factors; they assess children's performance on meaningful tasks directly related to the instruction provided. They blaze trails toward success on curricular outcomes by adjusting one or more areas of lessons. They differentiate *content* (what students learn), *process* (how they learn it), *product* (how students demonstrate content mastery), and *environment* (conditions that set the tone and expectations) (Tomlinson, 1999; Tomlinson & Strickland, 2005) depending on the needs they've identified through assessment.

Key Concepts

Summative assessment: assessment at the end of a teaching event (i.e. at the end of a unit of study). The assessment tool can be teacher made or a publisher's product.

Formative assessment: ongoing, in-the-moment assessment during the teaching of a lesson or unit.

Developmentally appropriate practice: a framework of principles and practices matched to the cognitive, social, and emotional level of learners.

DIFFERENTIATING CONTENT

Schumm, Vaughn, and Leavell (1994) offer a model, The Planning Pyramid, which outlines how to "plan for inclusionary instruction and meet the challenge of content coverage in general education classrooms for students with a broad range of academic needs" (p. 609). It's based on the principle that less is more—more time to uncover content using resources that students can and want to use. The pyramid allows teachers to distinguish what content all students must know.

This core becomes the focus for meaningful, differentiated instruction. There's also a sizable body of content most will learn anyway when presented in interesting and accessible ways. Based on interest and motivation more than ability, particular topics stimulate learners to delve deeper into content only some will learn (Shea, 2006). There is ample time to differentiate instruction, use time and space differently, continuously assess students' performance, and provide timely feedback when we put textbook content in its proper place on the pyramid (Shea, 2006; Tomlinson, 2001; Yatvin, 2004). Paths to the content at each level of the pyramid must be matched to the learners who travel them. Authentic assessment allows the teacher to create an effective path to core curricular standards—one well matched to the learner's interests and needs.

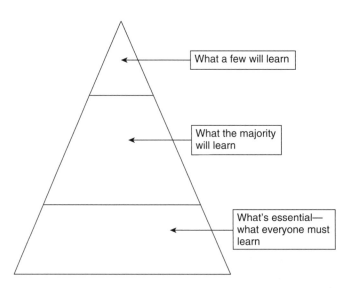

Figure 1.1 The Planning Pyramid: Levels of Content Learning for Unit of Study
Source Adapted from Schumm, Vaughn, and Leavell, 1994

Key Concept

Authentic assessment: measuring students' learning or skill development in the applications or performance of each in real world (authentic) tasks.

DIFFERENTIATING PROCESS

Children's interests, preferred ways of learning, and readiness influence the process (e.g. tasks and materials used) for their learning (Tomlinson, 1999). Vygotsky's (1978) theory proposes that learning is facilitated when the tasks children are expected to accomplish fall within their *zone of proximal development*. That zone is defined by what a learner can do with the help of a competent person (adult or peer), but cannot do alone. Teachers scaffold students' performances while they're in a zone (e.g. while learning a concept or skill), but teachers also need to scaffold learners *through* that zone (Dodge, 2005; Drapeau, 2004) and into the next level. The amount of scaffolding adjusts according to the child's changing needs and abilities (Berk & Winsler, 1995). Instruction in the zone is just right with regards to complexity, clarity, interest, and motivation. Tasks and materials are not too easy, creating boredom; they're neither too hard, causing frustration (Tobin, 2008).

Sousa (2001) concludes that moderate challenge is necessary for optimal learning. There's little satisfaction from accomplishing a mindless (without effort or thought) task aside from the fact that we got it done. But, a moderately challenging task requires a degree of preparation. We're ready to do it. Readiness (e.g. background knowledge and prerequisite skills) for a given task establishes the current range of the child's zone for it; readiness is determined by careful teacher observation and ongoing assessment (Allan & Tomlinson, 2000; Dodge, 2005; Vygotsky, 1978).

Tasks are designed to make concepts and skills in the zone accessible as well as appropriately interesting and challenging for students. This strengthens their self-esteem and motivation—essential ingredients related to improved learning and performance (Cruickshank, Brainer, & Metcalf, 1999; Murray, Shea, & Shea, 2004). Another factor in a Vygotskian learning framework is the concept of options; children make some decisions—within parameters of course—in a social contract model of learning. Pettig (2000) concludes, "choice validates a student's opinion and promotes self-efficacy" (p. 16).

DIFFERENTIATING PRODUCT

Children have options for how they will show what they know; differentiated products (e.g. journal entry, drawing, performance) demonstrate attainment of learning outcomes. Children's work samples reflect the multiple routes they've taken to reach curriculum outcomes while validating their understanding of core content (Tobin, 2008). Allowing children to decide how they'll demonstrate understanding honors individual interests; it increases students' engagement. Learners are more likely to take responsibility for choices made in a classroom where the tone implies respect for their ideas (Bess, 1997).

A CLASSROOM WITH A DIFFERENTIATED VIEW

A sense of community is quickly recognized in a differentiated classroom. It's an environment where students and teachers collaborate; it's safe to try or ask for help. And, there's an expectation that all can achieve (Tomlinson, 2001).

Fairness (equity) is redefined in the differentiated classroom; it's distinguished from the equality of sameness for all. "Fair means trying to make sure each student gets what she needs in order to grow and succeed" (Tomlinson, 2001, p. 23). It's difficult to address assessment, content, process, product, and the environment at once. That's why teachers typically start with one or two of these areas (Tomlinson & Strickland, 2005). However, assessment remains at the hub of the wheel; effectively observing and recording what learners currently know and can do is central to effectively differentiating in the other areas.

GETTING STARTED ON DIFFERENTIATING

Effective differentiation is complex (Tomlinson, 1999); but, researchers offer general principles to guide the process.

- Focus on the essential, core knowledge and skills in the content, creating paths for all to reach the same content standards (Pettig, 2000).
- Plan lessons based on diversity factors identified in the classroom (e.g. readiness, interest, ability, culture, language).

- Continuously monitor and document progress with meaningful assessments. These should incorporate authentic application of skills (e.g. authentic tasks) taught. For example, reading competency is assessed as children read from literature selections and retell what they understand; writing competency is assessed through a review of children's compositions (Shea, 2000; Shea et al., 2005).
- Analyze data collected and make appropriate instructional adjustments based on conclusions (Shea, 2000; Shea et al., 2005).
- Flexibly group students based on specific needs (Anderson, 2007; Rock, Gregg, Ellis, & Gable, 2008).

Greenwood, Tapia, Abbott, and Walton (2003) stress that a variety of grouping formats is essential in a differentiated classroom. Groups are always flexible, changing to accommodate the variations in learner readiness for a given topic or task. Ongoing assessment in the classroom allows the teacher to mindfully adjust groups in a timely manner. Flexible grouping ensures that curriculum is implemented with equity (Fahey, 2000).

Some children accept a project involving learning beyond lesson objectives; others are ready to work on tasks after initial instruction. Another group needs further demonstration in a small group while a few students need individualized reinforcement. "Each decision for grouping is based on making the appropriate match between the task and the student" (Dodge, 2005, p. 105). All decision making flows from valid assessment.

ASSESSMENT LEADS THE WAY

Meaningful pre-assessments provide essential information for planning differentiated lessons; ongoing assessment guides instructional modifications as the lesson is taught. While learners engage in activities, teachers observe and assess work products and performances. Ongoing (frequent) assessment keeps the teacher informed. Based on that knowledge, timely modifications are made in lessons (Earl, 2003).

Three dimensions of assessment are included when differentiating instruction for responsive teaching—determining students' background knowledge for the task, their responses to moderate challenges within it, and the measure of their performance against expected outcomes (Tomlinson, 1995). Running records (RR) provide data across those dimensions.

THE BOTTOM LINE

Differentiated teaching is student-aware teaching. The ultimate aim is to create focused, motivated, and take-charge learners (Tomlinson, 2008) who are more likely to realize their potential. Their achievement is enhanced when there's a just right balance of task difficulty, readiness level, and teacher support.

Ayers (2001) asks, "Given what I know, how should I teach this particular student?" (p. 109). Differentiating instruction helps teachers reach each child and move him forward. The body of research that reports significantly positive results with differentiated instruction in classrooms of diversity continues to grow (Rock et al., 2008).

Children deserve teachers who can provide an "appropriate response to a [each] unique encounter" in the teaching–learning relationship (Ayers, 2001, p. 17). Considering the principles of differentiation, RRs provide an authentic measure of the multi-faceted competencies that need to be seamlessly integrated by a reader. They meet the challenge in today's classrooms—the challenge to understand the uniqueness, the nonstandardness of each learner. That knowledge guides a teacher in planning for the right amount and kind of instruction needed at a particular moment.

EXTENDING THE DISCUSSION

- Think about the signs of differentiated instruction (responsive teaching) you've observed in classrooms or identify in your own classroom. How can these be refined or expanded based on the principles described in this chapter?
- Discuss why each area of differentiation—content, process, product, and environment—is essential to consider.
- Discuss: What information is essential for successful instructional differentiation?

2

RUNNING RECORDS AS AN AUTHENTIC
ASSESSMENT MEASURE

Big Ideas

What are authentic assessments?
Running records as authentic assessments
Curriculum based measures for ongoing assessment
Running records as formative and summative curriculum based
   measures
When and how to use running records for formative and
   summative assessment

AUTHENTIC ASSESSMENTS

Authenticity in assessment refers to the degree that the instrument used and the information gained from it measure performance of a skill in everyday use. If the task differs considerably from routine use of particular skills in the classroom, the information gained from it cannot effectively guide teaching those skills (Shea et al., 2005). Authentic assessments like RRs create a detailed picture of the learner's performance on target outcomes while—for the child—they're just another practice of what she does all the time (Shea, 2000, 2006).

RUNNING RECORDS AS AUTHENTIC
ASSESSMENT OF GROWTH IN READING

A RR is a method for establishing a student's "competence at a given moment in time with a specific level and type of book" (Shea, 2000, p. 10). RRs are regularly used to document the rapidly changing development of emergent readers. "It is the most efficient, quick way of gathering reliable data that is customized to the learner" (Shea, 2000, p. 5). Clay's (2004) protocol for RRs focuses on word reading and states that RRs provide "an assessment of [students'] text reading" (p. 3). This text outlines a procedure for *complete* RRs with young readers—one that includes data on reading *and* comprehension. This text describes a method for a RR assessment that also includes measures of text reading and learner self-initiated retelling. The video at the companion website and transcriptions of RRs completed by classroom teachers provide grist for extensive practice and discussions; these samples also allow teachers to "read" RRs taken by others as they would do when reviewing a student's reading history from earlier grades or previous schools. Teachers build comfort and confidence with the process before using RRs to measure children's ability to navigate any text. The protocol is easily woven into the fabric of day-to-day teaching, assessing, and planning.

RR data can be gathered on the spot, in the classroom, across content areas, and without prepackaged materials. This makes them superior to informal reading inventories (IRIs)—assessment packages that include short graded passages with prepared questions. Widely used IRIs have notable limitations.

Students easily become test savvy with IRIs. This happens when they overhear classmates read passages or after they've reread different levels of passages in subsequent testing sessions. In addition, IRI passages may not align with texts students are expected to read in the classroom. And, after all, we need to know how to help them read the texts used for instruction (Shea, 2006).

RRs have immediate relevancy; they provide meaningful and timely data for instruction because they're based on texts used in the classroom. Clay (2004) states that, "Having taken the record, teachers can review what happened immediately, leading to a teaching decision on the spot, or at a later time as they plan for next lessons" (p. 4).

Based on reliable information from RRs, teachers make appropriate adjustments in the genre and level of books used with students across all reading contexts. As a method of *dynamic assessment*, RRs focus attention on "both what the students can do individually and their potential growth as indicated by the interaction" (Dixon-Kraus, 1996, p. 152). The data from RRs allow immediate investigation of suspected problems in a learner's reading growth and provide specific information on his competency with texts he's expected to read. Records also provide an indication of students' mediated reading levels or "the highest level students can achieve [success] given adult support. These levels are higher than students' instructional reading levels and are more analogous to Vygotsky's concept of *emerging development*" (Dixon-Kraus, 1996, p. 153). Finally, we need to identify individual interests that motivate persistence, strengths that reveal what's already accomplished, and confusions that stop readers in their tracks, derailing comprehension, engagement, and, often, cooperative participation in classroom activities. And, we need to do this efficiently—in concert with classroom curriculum and materials before any meaningful differentiated instruction is possible.

Key Concepts

Dynamic assessment: assessment marked by continuous productive activity; more specifically it's one in which probes are used by the test administrator to explore the learner's responses more deeply, redirect him, or offer scaffolded support before measuring his response to such in-the-moment intervention.

Emerging development: evidence of success in a learner's assisted performance of a behavior at a certain level of difficulty. Although the initial demonstration is characterized as somewhat awkward, it reflects the learner's readiness for mediated instruction at that level.

DOCUMENT PROGRESS WITH CURRICULUM-BASED MEASURES

Along with universal screening, the *Response to Intervention* (RTI) process (see Preface) and responsive teaching begins with teacher observation during day-to-day instruction in the general education classroom. Although they often consult with colleagues, share ideas, and elicit suggestions, classroom teachers are responsible for delivering high quality, differentiated instruction to all students in their classroom (Drame & Xu, 2008).

Once potential at-risk students are identified, a system for continuous monitoring is initiated. Such monitoring may be brief (1–3 minutes per student) or slightly longer to determine a student's responsiveness to instruction. It involves a reliable, valid curriculum-based measure (CBM)—one associated with desired academic outcomes identified by the school for students at that level (Stecker, Fuchs, & Fuchs, 2005).

Although there's concern about the quality of particular instruments (Francis, Santi, Barr, Fletcher, Varisco, & Foorman, 2008), teachers understand that appropriate assessments pinpoint sources of confusion when administered effectively and accurately interpreted in a timely manner. Targeted instructional adjustments that follow have the potential to resolve most problems (Fuchs, Deno, & Mirkin, 1984). Reducing the number of children experiencing extended difficulties allows schools to direct resources and personnel toward those who continue to need additional help (VanDerHeyden, Witt, & Gilbertson, 2007).

Key Concept

Curriculum-based measure: an assessment tool that incorporates content associated with the curriculum in the classroom.

RUNNING RECORDS: FORMATIVE AND SUMMATIVE CURRICULUM-BASED MEASURES

RRs, discussed in subsequent chapters, meet the requirements for a valid, useful assessment tool when used effectively. They provide a reliable CBM of literacy acquisition. There isn't another assessment that provides as much information on a child's literacy development as a RR. Its efficient, timely, and reliable data are immediately available and highly useful for planning targeted instruction (Shea, 2000).

Fuchs and Fuchs (2006) recommend that in-the-classroom performances on curriculum-based objectives be the measure of responsiveness to instruction. RRs indicate a reader's fluency of decoding and depth of comprehension on a leveled text selection. Successful reading performance involves an integration of these multiple skills for text and meaning processing.

The information gleaned from a RR of the child's oral reading and self-initiated retelling has direct instructional utility. It's used to plan the next teaching step. Formative RRs provide information "on-the-spot, increasing the likelihood that materials, objectives, instruction, and learning activities are on target" (Shea, 2006, p. 16).

RRs assess multiple aspects of a child's literacy development (e.g. decoding skills, fluency, vocabulary knowledge, comprehension, and expressive language skills) in a reasonably short period of time. Accumulated RRs present evidence of growth or lack thereof in each component, as well as the child's ability to fluidly integrate skills.

A FORMATIVE RUNNING RECORD: WHEN AND WHY?

Formative RRs provide on-the-spot information, increasing the likelihood that materials, objectives, instruction, and learning activities are on target. Day-by-day, on the way to benchmark RRs, teachers want to know how students are navigating the texts they're being asked to use. This helps teachers plan effectively—differentiating tasks to match students' needs. When the priority is instruction guided by meaningful assessment data, teachers make time for RRs. "This kind of reflective interaction [RR session with the teacher] is possible within the daily life of the classroom" (Davenport & Lauritzen, 2002, p. 110). And, the information is immediately useful. If students are comfortable with the material, teachers allow more independence. If it's challenging, they provide more guidance.

To determine students' level of comfort or challenge with particular texts, teachers take a formative RR. They call these *on-the-run* RRs; such RRs are used to determine a reader's competency with primary classroom texts or ancillary ones the teacher wishes to use when augmenting a unit of study. In this situation:

- the passage can be (but doesn't have to be) a familiar one. It may have been heard, previously read, or previewed;
- a smaller section of text might be read;
- the teacher consistently follows standard RR procedures, but often uses prompting when readers stumble. This is done to determine whether the prompted reader can apply strategies that he's not self-initiating. If the prompting is *heavy* (nearly giving the word), the teacher scores the prompt as an error even when the reader eventually gets the word. The reader hasn't acquired the strategy; it needs to be retaught and reinforced. If the prompt is *light* (barely suggestive), the teacher doesn't score the prompt as an error. Self-initiated

use of strategies needs to be encouraged; independence requires the ability to successfully initiate and apply strategies effectively across situations.

Formative RRs allow teachers to monitor a reader's pulse with any text. What they learn guides *in-the-moment* instruction and fuels plans for an appropriate next lesson (Shea, 2006).

A BENCHMARK OR SUMMATIVE RUNNING RECORD: WHEN AND WHY?

RRs can be used both as a *benchmark* measure and a *summative* assessment. Results are used to determine the learner's level of performance at a given point in time and to compare that to an expected target score. When RRs are taken for this purpose, Shea (2006) suggests the following protocol.

- The reading passage is new. It hasn't been previously heard or read by the student.
- Standard procedures for administering and scoring the record are followed.
- The reader works independently throughout the assessment.

Any teacher can take a benchmark, summative RR. The classroom teacher, literacy specialist, or resource teacher regularly takes benchmark RRs to determine students' overall level of performance at a given point in time. But, in between benchmark points, teachers need to know how students are faring with texts they're required to use day-by-day in the classroom.

Both type of RRs are important. Each has a place in guiding, documenting, and reporting students' growth toward learning outcomes.

THE NEXT STEP

Chapter 3 introduces the marking codes for each kind of miscue that readers make. It also further explores when and why teachers use RRs for formative and benchmark data. Following the suggested timeline for implementation of RRs allows graduated practice with the codes and protocols. Both teachers and children become familiar with the process, reducing stressful responding and adding to the reliability of data collected.

EXTENDING THE DISCUSSION

- Discuss current in-the-classroom reading assessment you've observed or the kind of assessment used in your own classroom. Consider how helpful it is in informing the most efficient next step in instruction for readers.
- Brainstorm the information you would expect to receive from a RR. Discuss whether this is more or less than the information obtained from currently used measures. How would it differ?

Part II
Running Records Step-by-Step
*Assessment that Informs Differentiated
Reading Instruction*

3

ASSESSING READING ACCURACY

Big Ideas

Assessment-teaching cycle

Communicating progress in reading

The running record process—recognizing strengths, providing feedback, using data, identifying reading levels

Understanding running record codes, taking the record, scoring results

Using data

RUNNING RECORDS INFORM THE ASSESSMENT–TEACHING CYCLE

Yet a funny thing happens on the way to those final assessments: day-to-day learning takes place. I am certain that, in education, evaluation needs to pay more attention to the systematic observation of learners who are on their way to those final assessments.

(Clay, 1987, p. 1)

Step-by-step monitoring (assessment) of children's learning provides insights that allow teachers to give appropriate support in a timely way. It's the stitch in time that saves nine—an essential for responsive, differentiated teaching. To determine the most appropriate next step in literacy instruction, the teacher observes a child as he reads and shares an understanding of the text. A process for documenting this observation is called taking a RR.

RRs reveal skills and strategies the child uses to decode, comprehend, and interpret different kinds and levels of text read orally or silently (Shea, 2000, 2006). The process of taking a RR becomes nonthreatening when the teacher explains that the purpose is to direct her teaching. She begins by saying something like, "I'll listen to your reading and retelling so I can make notes on the good things you're doing and decide how I can help you." Assessment anxiety seldom inhibits performance or deflates scores when the task begins this way (Davenport & Lauritzen, 2002).

The teacher and student talk about the performance after the record is taken, discussing strengths and areas of need. In this "teaching conversation" (Davenport & Lauritzen, 2002, p. 109) the teacher models how to be reflective about reading by commenting on effective strategies she observed, investigating the thinking behind miscues, or examining the fullness of the retelling (Shea, 2000, 2006).

This debriefing develops insights about the performance (Goodman & Marek, 1996); it invites clarification. Readers build skill in *metacognitive* talk (articulating one's thinking) and move toward self-initiated reflection (Davenport & Lauritzen, 2002). Gradually, readers begin to take control.

Effective tools, systematically applied in the assessment process, are integral to the overall validity of documentations for responsive, differentiated teaching. RRs meet the criteria (Davenport & Lauritzen, 2002). Consistency across settings is also achieved, leading to clearer communication about students' progress. That communication extends to parents as well. Keeping them informed strengthens the home–school relationship.

COMMUNICATING WITH PARENTS

Parents want timely information on their child's progress. Get them on board by explaining how you're using RRs to assess children's reading growth (Shea et al., 2005). A sample letter to parents can be found at the companion website.

It helps if this is a schoolwide initiative. Teachers can collaborate to plan a program that will inform parents. Invite children to come along; they can add to the conversation by sharing their experiences. A good idea would be to have videotapes of children reading and retelling—like the one at the companion website. The audience would enjoy watching the process together. The images are worth a thousand words.

THE RUNNING RECORD PROCESS

In the context of assessment, RRs refer to the ongoing and complete recording of a child's words as she reads and retells the story (Clay, 1993a). RRs are used to consistently observe, record, and analyze a child's reading performance. The RR codes information for analysis and documents competencies the child has acquired (Clay, 1993a). Notations are detailed enough to provide a multi-layered account of oral reading, comprehension, fluency, and problem-solving skills.

Like learning any new skill, taking an accurate RR may appear daunting at first, but it's very doable when you allow yourself an opportunity to practice and take advantage of support systems. Soon, RRs become a routine event in the classroom (Davenport & Lauritzen, 2002; Shea, 2000, 2006). The companion website has a timetable for starting the RR process in your classroom. You can begin early, proceed gradually, and have meaningful data for the first quarterly report.

To take a RR, the teacher sits in a quiet area with the reader while other children work. This work could include independent reading and writing, center work, or group projects. Other texts suggest efficient classroom protocols and organization that allow teachers to schedule time with individuals while other students are meaningfully engaged (Boushey & Moser, 2006, 2009; Collins, 2004). The child reads aloud as the teacher takes a record, coding what the child reads and evaluating comprehension from the child's story retelling (telling what it was all about). After analyzing well-defined markers of literacy knowledge, the teacher meaningfully plans the next instructional step for the reader.

RUNNING RECORDS CELEBRATE STRENGTHS

When the child has finished reading and retelling, the teacher discusses the record in a teaching conversation by giving a compliment that illustrates what the child did well.

TEACHER: Your reading was smooth. You grouped words together this time and made it sound like talking. I like the way you used expression in the scary part.

RUNNING RECORDS PROVIDE THE CHILD
WITH IMMEDIATE FEEDBACK

After pointing out strengths, the teacher provides sensitively stated comments (feedback) on noted areas of difficulty. The teacher discusses one or two errors with the child (teaching points), explaining how each could have been corrected. The choices made for the teaching conversation "are crucial to the reading growth of students" (Davenport & Lauritzen, 2002, p. 112) because they describe reading strategies in context, bringing the process to a conscious level. For example:

TEACHER: I notice that you were a successful problem-solver when you didn't know a word. Let's explore another solution. You skipped this word when reading. Here's where I marked that. Do you know it?

CHILD: No.

T: How can you figure it out?

C: Sound it out.

T: You *can* look at the letters and think about the sounds for those letters. What else can you think about? What will help you figure it out?

C: Use the CLUNK list (see Figure 3.1). Mmm … think about what's happening. Look at the picture.

T: Those are good places for clues that you can match with the sound clues. Reread this part and use those ideas to figure out the word.

C: The beaver had strong, mmm … /sh/ … mmm … oh, I know—sharp … teeth, because … look … they're pointed in the picture and he's cutting the branch with it!

T: Good for you! You thought about what word could describe his teeth and looked at the illustration for clues to match the starting /sh/ sound.

Sometimes teachers use this kind of teachable moment for an on-the-spot mini lesson that emphasizes the importance of integrating cues (clues) for word solving. These are discussed in Chapter 7.

The teacher might say something like the following.

TEACHER: While you're reading, be sure to keep thinking—think about the information the author is sharing or the story he's telling. Use pictures and charts on the page. This will make it easier to figure out words. The word can't be any word in the world. It has to make sense and sound right—like the way we talk. When your brain expects to see certain words, your eyes will recognize the one that is there much faster. When you see the author's word, check that it makes sense, sounds right, and has the right letters to be the word you think it is.

A Strategy for Word Solving

Provide abundant demonstrations of this CLUNK strategy before you invite children to use it independently. Post it in the classroom as a reference.

Make parents aware of strategies you're modeling and expecting children to use.

A CLUNK is a word that stops you in your tracks.

What do you do when you meet a **CLUNK**? You …

1. Say mmm … and keep going to the end of the sentence with the CLUNK while thinking about meaning. Reread the sentence with the CLUNK while thinking about the meaning clues you now have.

2. "Crash into" the CLUNK. Make your mouth say the sounds for the beginning of the CLUNK while you look across the rest of the word and check all the letters/parts.

3. When you've figured out the word, reread the sentence it's in before continuing to read.

4. If you still haven't figured it out, put in a word that would make sense, reread the sentence, and, then, continue to read.

5. Ask someone about the CLUNK word when you're finished reading to learn a new word.

Figure 3.1 The CLUNK Test

As a caveat, keep mini lessons mini. Less is more. Many mini lessons stimulate learning leaps. There's a decoding mini lesson at the companion website. When reviewing it, notice that it has all the essential elements for a plan with a logical sequence (Hoyt, 2000). Don't let your mini lessons become maxi ones. Many mini lessons will lead to big steps in learners' growth.

USING RUNNING RECORDS

RRs, accompanied by story retellings, portray a child's meaning making and use of problem-solving strategies when reading. Anecdotal notes stimulate rich discussions that allow meaningful goal setting.

Plan time to listen to readers and take rich, useful notes in response to the questions offered in Figure 3.2. Your comments should identify specific reader behaviors in clear terms. The publisher's website has a list of additional reading behaviors that one might typically observe. Use it as a starting point for your own anecdotal notes.

Accumulated RRs create a record of literacy growth over time. Information gained from them can be used:

- to identify a child who needs special assistance;
- to determine whether a particular book is appropriate;
- to flexibly group children with similar needs for instruction.

As discussed in Chapter 2, RRs provide formative and summative assessment depending on how they are administrated.

A GOOD FIT FOR LEARNING

RRs are taken to determine a good fit of text to readers. The record establishes the difficulty level of a particular text for a particular reader at the time it's taken. It could fall in one of three levels. The child can read *independent level* text by himself. Texts at this level are appropriate for Drop Everything And Read (DEAR) time when children read independently. The child can read *instructional level* text with support from the teacher and/or peers. Texts at this level offer moderate challenge; they should be used in guided reading. *Frustrational level* texts are too hard for the child to read right now even with help from others. Texts at this level can be read aloud because children's listening levels are usually higher than their reading levels. Read-alouds of high interest texts motivate, build background knowledge and vocabulary, and offer a preview of literature that awaits the growing reader.

Selecting an appropriate text for the RR is critically important. The book should be a text at the child's instructional level—one that will be moderately challenging and require her to apply known strategies for word solving. Introduce children to the concept of reading levels; emphasize that a book that is too hard right now will be instructional as they learn more about reading. It will eventually be easy.

THE GOLDILOCKS TEST

Help students classify a text's difficulty level for themselves using the Goldilocks test. See Figure 3.3. It can be enlarged and posted in the room.

1. Tell the children what will be happening during the oral reading session and why. Explain that while you and individual students work together, the rest of the class will work independently. Go over any ground rules for acceptable activities and behaviors.
2. Post a weekly schedule of the reading conferences in a central location in the room. Start with one per day. After a few weeks, you may feel that you can complete two per day.
3. Invite each reader to join you in a quiet area of the room. Have him bring a book that matches the Goldilocks "just-right" category. It may be a book that the class is reading for its literature study, a book the child has been reading, or a book you've read to the class. Most importantly, it must offer some, but not too much challenge.
4. While the child reads the book aloud, take notes. Use the guide that describes a variety of reading behaviors and strategies you might notice. (See "Examples of Anecdotal Notes for Observations on a Child's Oral Reading" found at the website.)
5. Talk briefly with the child about the content of the book (a retell); be sure he's comprehended it.
6. Discuss the notes you took while the child read. Encourage him to comment on your observations and add any of his own.
7. As soon as possible, revisit the anecdotal notes you took during the session and during your post-reading conversation with the child. Add any thoughts and conclusions about the child's performance.
8. Plan weekly meetings with one or more colleagues, including resource teachers. Share your anecdotal notes; invite reactions and alternative interpretations. The following questions will guide your discussions and stimulate conversation:
   - Was the child comfortable and confident?
   - Did he understand what he read? Fully or just the gist of it? Where was the confusion?
   - Did many errors cause the meaning to be lost? What caused the errors?
   - Did he make connections with background knowledge and earlier reading?
   - Did he read smoothly? How accurately did he read words?
   - Did he use multiple clues (cues) to figure out words? What were they?
   - Did he attempt to self-correct? What strategies did he use? How successful was he?
9. Add insights from meetings with your colleagues to your notes. File your notes and reports in children's portfolios.
10. Follow this plan until you've completed anecdotal notes on one session with each child.

Figure 3.2 A 10 Step Plan for Anecdotal Records

Choose a "just right" book to read to the teacher.

Too Easy—My independent level

> I know all or most of the words in the book or on the page.
> I know a lot about this topic.
> I've read the book many times before.

Just Right—My instructional level

> The book looks interesting and I know something about the topic.
> I know most of the words in the book or on a page.
> There's someone to help when I need it.

Too Hard—My frustrational level

> There are a lot of words I don't know.
> I don't know a lot about this topic.
> There's no one to read this book to me.

Figure 3.3 Goldilocks (and the Three Bears) Test
Source Adapted from Ohlhausen and Jepsen, 1992, as cited in Tompkins, 2010, p. 344–345

The Goldilocks Test uses a finger up method. As the child skims the book, he notes the number of words on a page or in a paragraph that he doesn't know by putting up a finger for each. If four or five fingers go up, the book is probably too hard (frustrational) right now. If two or three go up, it's probably just right (instructional) for guided reading and doing a RR. And, if only one or zero fingers go up, it's probably an easy book and appropriate for independent reading time.

Have books in the classroom clearly labeled by difficulty, type, and topic. Have some leveled books set aside for benchmark RR. These will be ones children have not read before the RR is taken. Most publishers provide information on book levels (e.g. letter level, grade level, interest level). You can also go to http://kansas.bookconnect.com to find levels for many familiar books, use Microsoft Office tools on your computer, or go to websites that allow you to type in text and evaluate its readability (e.g. http://www.addedbytes.com/lab/readability-score or http://www.online-utility.org/english/readability_test_and_improve.jsp).

BE FLEXIBLE ABOUT BOOK SELECTION
AND NUMBER OF WORDS

Sometimes, teachers have children read a familiar or unfamiliar text they've selected based on a specific purpose for taking the record; this can occur whether the RR is used as a formative or benchmark assessment. At other times, teachers ask the reader to select a text for the RR. Either way, it should be a book that has some hard words in it (instructional). Tell the reader, "I need to see what strategies you use when you meet a word you don't know right away. This will help me plan my teaching." When children understand the teacher's purpose, they participate without feeling anxious.

The length of texts the child reads can vary. Passages will be shorter for children at the emergent level, but, as a rule, keep 100 words as an approximate lower limit. Allow children to go beyond 100 words and even complete a text when they're really involved in it. Fluency and comprehension naturally improve as readers begin to grasp the overall gist of a text. If the text is a picture book and the reader appears comfortable, let him finish it. If it's a chapter book, stop at an appropriate pause in the action—at a point that allows for a substantive retelling. However, it's better not to tell the reader where to stop until he gets there. Otherwise, he'll rush to that place.

TAPE THE SESSION

Be prepared to audio or video tape the session. See teaching tip #3 at the companion website. Taping the RR (audio only or video) serves many purposes. You can use tapes to verify your marking. You can also assess fluency when listening to the tapes later. The number of words read correctly per minute (WCPM) can be calculated from the tape. When done this way, the child doesn't feel pressured to rush as he might when competing with a stopwatch. He didn't even know the measure would be calculated; the score is more valid, reflecting a true level. Fluency is discussed in Chapter 5 and there is an explanation of how to calculate the number of words read correctly per minute from the RR as one factor of fluency. Taping the RR has other benefits as well. When teachers share these tapes with other teachers or parents, they spark conversation about the clearly revealed strengths and needs of the reader. Meaningful interventions can be planned based on these discussions.

UNDERSTANDING THE CODES

Through coding a RR, teachers gather significant information on how well a child reads words (text processing). While the mechanics of taking the record seems overwhelming at first, do not despair. The shorthand marks, or codes, will help you quickly record all the details you notice. See Figure 3.4.

You'll be able to capture an entire reading episode for later analysis. Soon the marks will be second nature and you'll be able to keep up with a fluent reader. Remember, the tape allows you to review the child's performance; revise the record if you missed something. See teaching tip #4 at the companion website related to recording oral readings. Discuss the idea with colleagues.

Use the codes and procedures to record a student's text-processing behaviors. In this chapter, scoring guidelines are included for each code and an illustration of how they look in a RR. There's also a summary of the codes at the companion website that can be printed out.

It's important to note that you do not need a script of the text read to understand what the child said and follow the markings when analyzing a previously completed RR. Nor do you need to write out a script of the child's reading when taking a RR. See Figures 3.5 and 3.6. You'll find additional examples like the one in Figure 3.5 as well as a blank form for taking a RR at the companion website. The video segment at the website does not show a script of the child's reading. Copies of the text read for all RR samples are not provided at the website. Although having the context of the passage can be helpful in discerning a possible logic for some miscues, teachers often need to "read" a RR report (with coding) and evaluate the reading performance without a copy of the text read (i.e. when reviewing previous records for a child). Words read correctly, as indicated by checks, are not typically a concern; areas of strength and needs in word reading (decoding) and comprehension can be determined by the coding process on the RR form, rubrics, and checklists. You can also get a copy of books used in this text to compare the RRs line by line.

After the oral reading, retelling, and conference are completed, thank the child and direct her to an activity in the classroom. Later in the day you can score errors, tally results, and add comments. You can also analyze the child's miscues. Miscue analysis is discussed in Chapter 4.

1. Correct word: Check marks are recorded for words read correctly.

Mark every word read accurately with a check. The checks must match the number of words in each line of text. Record page (or paragraph) numbers for later reference. The record should match the text—line-by-line, page-by-page.	Page 1 Sometimes it looked √ √ √ like spilt milk. √ √ √ But it wasn't spilt milk. √ √ √ √ √ From: *It Looked Like Spilt Milk* by Charles Shaw, 1988

2. Incorrect word (miscue): Record the incorrect word the reader said with the text word under it. These are called substitution errors. Substitution errors are analyzed for semantic, syntactic, and graphophonemic (letter/sound) acceptability.

Score incorrect words as errors.	reader <u>horse</u> text house

3. Trials/attempts: Record each incorrect attempt above the correct word.

Sounding out may be recorded in lower case letters, (c-a-t) **Score unsuccessful attempts as errors.**	reader <u>horse</u>— h..h..h— home text house

4. Reader's self-corrections: Mark as sc. Record each self-correction by crossing out the miscue and writing the letters sc above it.

When scoring, these are figured into the self-correction frequency but not the accuracy percent.	sc reader ~~when~~ text where

5. Word omissions: Record an empty circle above the text word or write down the omitted word and circle it.

Score the omitted words as an error.	reader ◯ or (green) text green

Figure 3.4 A List of Running Record Codes
Source Adapted from Clay, 1993a; Goodman and Burke, 1972; Johns, 2008; Leslie and Caldwell, 2011; Shea, 2000

6. Word insertion: Record any inserted word by writing it above a caret.

Score insertions as errors.	the ∧

7. Teacher-given word: Insert **T**, which stands for *told*.

If the teacher tells the reader the word because the child is stuck, it is marked with a **T**. The teacher might first suggest, *Try the strategies you know to figure it out* (i.e. **CLUNK** strategies). **Score T words as errors.**	reader <u>horse</u> text house — **T**

8. Appeal for help: Write **A** when the child appeals for help. Write the miscue made if the child makes an attempt when prompted to try. Record **T** if the word is then teacher-given.

When the reader asks for help, the teacher might suggest, *You try it. Use the strategies you know.* Then, the teacher can observe the reader's ability to apply strategies taught and practiced. If the child is still unsuccessful, the word is teacher-given (**T**). **Score words given as errors.**	Reader — A — <u>horse</u> Text house **T**

9. Start Over: Record **SO** with the repeated text in the bracket.

If the reader seems to be totally confused and is making a series of errors, stop him and suggest that he start over. Show him where to begin again. The repeated text may be more than one line. **Score the start over as one error since it was a teacher-directed repeat. Any corrections made are then scored as self-corrections.**	reader text reader text	⌐ sc <s>Somewhere</s> <u>they</u> Sometimes it sc ∅ <u> </u> like	sc <s>liked</s> looked sc ∅ <u> </u> spilt √	**SO** ⌐

Figure 3.4 (Continued)

10. Repetition: Write ←---------- R to indicate a repetition.

Repetitions often result in self-corrections. If the child repeats the same words several times, a sub number tells how many. The arrow is drawn back to the beginning of the repetition. If many repetitions are interrupting fluency and inhibiting comprehension, that should be noted in overall comments on the reading. **Do not count repetitions as errors.**	Examples: text: Sometimes it looked √ √ √ ←----R text: The boy ran to the new swing. sc Ø √ √ √ √ √ new √ ←----------------------R₂

11. Hesitations: Write H to indicate a hesitation in decoding.

Mark significant hesitations (3–4 seconds). It reflects choppy reading and a need for closer analysis in word recognition. Readers sometimes hesitate when they're anticipating difficulty with an upcoming word. They may be rereading silently to get a running start at the suspected unknown word. **A hesitation doesn't count as an error.**	text: The tail is especially long. H...es.....√ √ √ √ especially √

12. Reverse word order: Use a loop [⌢] to identify words reversed.

Sometimes readers reverse the order of words in the text. Often they are following a previous pattern in the text or a familiar pattern of speech, and the reversal doesn't interrupt meaning. **Score reversals as two errors — one for each word since RRs are coded as a word-to-word match.**	Text: You can ride along with me any time you want, said Dad. √ √ √ √ √ √ √ √ √ said Dad

Figure 3.4 (Continued)

13. Errors with contractions: Code as two errors—a substitution and insertion or a substitution and omission.

Sometimes readers will say the two words a contraction stands for or say a contraction for two words in text. Coding always maintains a word-to-word match. **Score these as two errors.** Although this doesn't interrupt meaning, it affects the score. Caution the reader to notice the author's words.	reader <u>do</u> <u>not</u> text don't ∧ reader <u>don't</u> text do (not)

14. Attempts with partial result or nonword: Record the attempt above the correct word.

A reader may attempt a word but come up with a partial word or nonword. It's important to record what the attempt is. This reveals word and letter/sound knowledge as well as strategies that the reader is trying. **Score incorrect attempts as errors.**	reader <u>disappoint</u> text disappointment reader <u>dispotent</u> text disappointment

15. Variations on the text word: Record the reader's spoken word over the correct text word.

The reader may make an error involving a sound, grammatical, or vocabulary variation resulting from regional, cultural, or dialectical differences. Or, he may pronounce a word incorrectly because of difficulty with articulation. **Dialectical speech differences should not be counted as errors unless the teacher knows that these are not common to the reader's speech in other situations.**	Reader <u>mus</u> <u>wuv</u> Text must love

Figure 3.4 (Continued)

16. Changing the correct word to an incorrect one: Record a slash through the check mark for that word and write the miscue above it.

Sometimes readers abandon the correct reading of a word and reread it incorrectly. When reviewing the record with the reader, explore why the change was made—what thoughts went through the reader's mind. **This change is scored as an error.**	Text: It was probably a mistake. √ √ ~~possibly~~ √ √ probably

17. Pronunciation shifts: Record the word as the child pronounced it (showing his emphasis and how the meaning was changed) above the text.

When reviewing the record with the reader, find out if he knew the meaning of the desired word, but simply used the incorrect pronunciation. **Pronunciation shifts that change the word count as errors.**	reader <u>rec' ord</u> (an account) text re cord (to note)

18. Teacher prompt: P, plus individual codes showing a teacher-suggested strategy—one that's been taught. If the reader gets the word with a little nudging, it is marked with a **P** (which notes what kind of prompt it was) and a check. If the reader misses the word, it is scored as an error. If the teacher has to provide the word, it is marked either **A-T** (appeal, then teacher-given) or **T** (teacher-given with no appeal). Specific prompts are given when the RR is used as formative assessment. It reveals whether the reader can use strategies when prompted, but just isn't self-initiating them or deciding which to use. However, when the RR is a benchmark, I prompt to use strategies, but don't direct toward specific ones. I want to assess what the reader can do independently.

Teacher-prompted strategy codes	What the teacher suggested to the reader
P-cc	Try context clues
P-pc	Try picture clues
P-sc	Try letter/sound clues

Figure 3.4 (Continued)

If the reader appeals for help, but isn't ready to use word identification strategies independently, the teacher may prompt to use a certain strategy (see above).	Examples:
This intervention allows the teacher to determine that the child knows strategies and how to apply them, but is unable to initiate them or decide which would be most efficient in a particular situation.	She worked at the library after school.
If the accuracy score is within the independent range, but several prompts were given, the text may still be at the reader's instructional level.	The spaceship landed right in front of his house.

For "She worked at the library after school.":

$$\underline{A... P\text{-}pc\; \checkmark}$$

√ √ √ √ library   √

√

For "The spaceship landed right in front of his house.":

H...P-pc..sc

$$\underline{\phi}$$

√ spaceship√ √ √

←-------------------R

√ √ √ √

I have used these prompting codes effectively with running records, but they are not found in traditional running records or Informal Reading Inventories (IRIs).

19. Punctuation omissions: There are differences of opinion regarding the scoring of punctuation omissions. Leslie & Caldwell (2011) do not count repetitions, hesitations, and omissions of punctuation because they tend to be scored unreliably. Johns (2008) recommends that the teacher count the omission of words and punctuation in a tally of total errors. Punctuation errors should be noted. The degree to which they interrupt fluency and appear to inhibit efficient comprehension should also be noted.

20. Print Conventions: With emergent readers, note directional movement on the page (left page first, left to right—L to R , return sweep, top to bottom—T to B) tracking of the print, and accuracy in one-to-one word matching. This can be done with symbols

(←----, ----→), letters (L to R, T to B) and words.

Figure 3.4 (Continued)

RR for *Arthur Writes a Story*

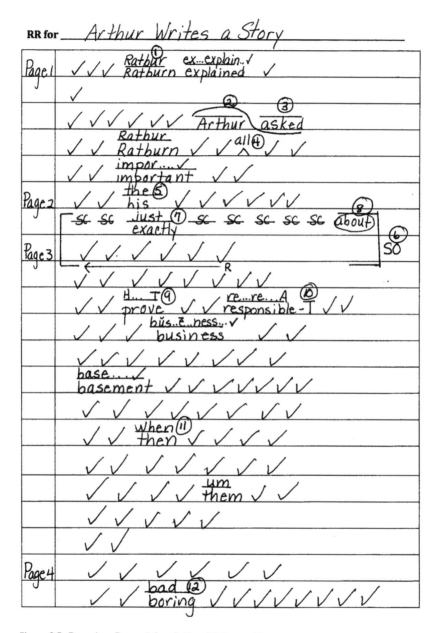

Figure 3.5 Running Record for *Arthur Writes a Story*

RR for _Arthur Writes a Story (cont.)_

Page 4 (cont.)	✓ ✓ ✓ ✓ ✓ ✓ ✓ (dull) ⑬
	✓ ✓ ✓ ✓ ✓ ✓ bad ⑭
	✓ ✓ boring ⑯ ✓ ✓
	✓ ✓ w...✓ ✓ ✓ said ⑮ I✓ ⑯ would ⑰ ✓ ✓
	were Suggested I'd ∧
	✓ ✓ ✓ ✓
	17 miscues 174 −17 = 157 words read correctly
	174 words in 157 ÷ 174 = 90 % accuracy
	passage
Notes:	Several words were decoded with closer
	analysis – i.e. explained, important, basement.
	He omitted the second line on page 2 and
	was directed to go back to it (so - start over).
	I think he was just anxious to read
	Arthur's story. We discussed the meaning
	of dull. He understood what boring meant,
	but didn't recognize the word. Most
	miscues did not interrupt meaning. He
	understood and enjoyed the story. He
	talked about caring for his dog and
	about friends giving you ideas for
	stories.

Figure 3.5 (Continued)

Steps	Commentary
Tally the number of errors and correct words. I count **all** errors. When only errors that change meaning are counted, scores become less reliable due to differences in opinion.	The section of the book read had 174 words. The child made 17 errors or miscues (each is numbered). He read 157 out of 174 words correctly.
Note that trials that are eventually correct do not count as errors.	The reader made repeated tries at words (i.e. *explained, important, business*) before eventually getting them. These are not errors. With closer analysis, the child can figure them out, but they are not sight words.
Note that insertions add errors. A reader could have more errors than there are words on a line. However, the reader cannot have more errors than words on a page. If the error count for a page does exceed the number of words on it, use the latter as the count of errors for that page.	The reader inserted the word *all* (error #4). It didn't interfere with meaning.
If a word, line, or sentence is omitted, count each word as an error. If a page is omitted because two were turned at once, don't count the missed words as errors. Adjust the total number of possible words when you're calculating the accuracy percent.	The reader missed the second line on page 2 in his hurry to get to Arthur's story. When he read the title of the story, I realized his omission and asked him to go back, Start Over (SO—#6) at line 2 on page 2, and continue reading from there. He read most of the line correctly. This resulted in three errors (#6—the SO, #7—a substitution of *just* for *exactly*, and #8—the omission of *about*) instead of 9 errors for each omitted word in the line.
Count a repeated substitution for the same word (e.g. home for house, lady for woman) as an error <u>each time</u>. Consistent substitutions of proper nouns (e.g. Timmy for Tommy), however, are only counted <u>the first time</u>. If a different proper noun is substituted (e.g. changed to Tammy for Tommy) an additional error is scored.	The reader read *Ratbur* for *Ratburn* (the teacher's name). It only counted the first time (error #1). He substituted *bad* for *boring* two times (errors #12 and #14) and each time an error was counted.
There is a one-to-one count of words on the page and utterances by the reader. If the child reads two words for one (i.e. two words for a contraction), two errors are scored. If a reader reads an entire phrase incorrectly, each word misread counts as an error. If it is self-corrected, each word corrected becomes a self-correction.	The child read *I would* for *I'd*. I scored the substitution and the insertion as errors. Do for don't is scored as a substitution and not is scored as an insertion (errors #16 and #17).

Figure 3.6 Scoring the Oral Reading of *Arthur Writes a Story*—Step-by-Step

Steps	Commentary
When a word is read as two words (i.e. *a/way* instead of *away*), it is regarded as a pronunciation error and not counted unless what is said is matched to another word (i.e. *away with* is read *a way with*).	
If the child is asked to start over, that counts as a single error. The rereading—not the first reading—is scored. It is advisable to have the reader start over when he has significantly lost meaning and accuracy. The number of self-corrections that follow the rereading offsets the additional error.	I asked the reader to start over at page 2, line 2 and counted the SO as an error (#6). I scored errors #7 and #8 based on his rereading of the line.
Dialectal or characteristic ways of saying words are not scored as errors.	The reader said *um* for *them* (page 3, line 10). This was typical of his speech. He meant *them*.
If the reader begins to invent the text, stop scoring it as a running record, but continue to take notes on the quality of the inventing. Observe how well the invention matches the gist of the text and illustrations on the page, the reader's use of expression, and any attempts of one-to-one word matching. Share your observations with the reader.	Feedback must be positive, but truthful. Celebrate what the reader can do. Let him know that you believe growth is continuing. If you stop recording, he'll immediately feel a sense of failure. You might say, "You did a great job continuing the story in your own way. You made the story match the pictures on the page and go in the order the author intended. And you used lots of expression. When we practice more, you'll be able to read the whole book in the author's words." If possible, find an easier book so that the child can read the actual words.

Figure 3.6 (Continued)

Key Concepts

Miscues: errors in reading.

Miscue analysis: an analysis of the reader's substitution errors to determine their semantic, syntactic, and/or letter/sound appropriateness (similarity) to the text word.

KEEPING SCORE

You need to take four types of calculations into consideration when scoring the oral reading. The first three are accuracy (as shown in the Arthur example), error-frequency, and self-correction rate (as shown in the examples at the companion website). Numbers are rounded to the nearest whole in calculating the first three scores. The fourth score, fluency, is discussed in Chapter 5. Figure 3.7 shows the blank form for taking the RR. This form and another for an informal "taking a reader's pulse" type of RR—one used spontaneously to check how well the reader is navigating a particular book—can be found at the companion website. Figure 3.8 explains where information about the reader, text, and scores described in the next part of this chapter are recorded. Chapter 4 will go into further detail recording miscue analysis on the form.

ACCURACY

Compute the accuracy rate to find the percent of words the reader read correctly. This figure helps you determine a child's word reading levels and is a key component in evaluating her overall reading ability. To compute word-reading accuracy, simply divide the number of words read correctly (the number of words in the selection minus the number of errors) by the total number of words in the selection. This gives a measure of word recognition competency. This score has been calculated for *Arthur Writes a Story* and the other RR samples at the companion website.

> **Example:** If the text had a total of 182 words and the child made 7 errors, calculate that 175 words were read correctly (182–7 = 175). Then, compute the percent of accuracy by dividing 175 by 182: 175/182 = 96% accuracy (rounded to nearest whole percent).

The table in Figure 3.9 gives cut-off accuracy percents for independent, instructional, and frustrational level classifications. The qualitative criteria for comprehension are discussed in Chapter 6.

RELATING READING ACCURACY TO READING LEVELS

Teachers must know the child's current reading levels to be sure that the child has an appropriate book. A RR provides this information. Using the calculated percent of accuracy and the matching reading levels in Figure 3.9, you can determine whether the chosen text is at this reader's independent, instructional, or frustrational level. You can also

Reader_____Gr. ___ Date_____
Recorder_____
Text Read_____
____Familiar____Unfamiliar Genre_____Text Level_____
Accuracy ____% SC %: _____ E freq.: _____ Fluency Av. _____ WCPM _____
Comprehension_____full_____satisfactory_____fragmented / or _____% on questions
Reading level for this text:_____independent _____instructional _____frustrational
Comments_____
_____
_____
_____
_____

Page	Marking for text read	# E	# SC	Error match		
				M	S	L-S

Figure 3.7 Running Record Recording Form

Page	Marking for text read (cont.)	# E	# SC	Error match		
				M	S	L-S

Figure 3.7 (Continued)

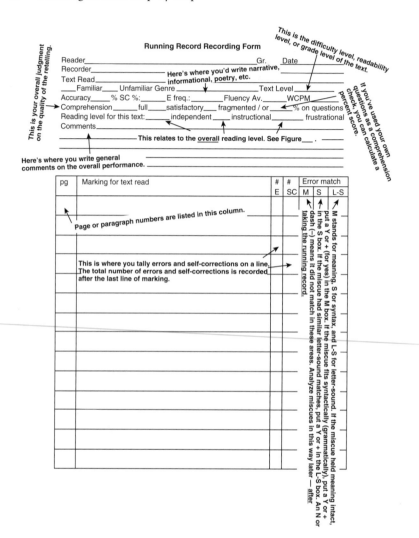

Figure 3.8 Guide for Recording Information and Scores on the Running Record Form

factor in comprehension as noted on the chart. Both accuracy and comprehension need to be considered when matching a child with a text. Assessing comprehension is discussed in Chapter 6.

There can be differences in reading level attained with different types of texts (e.g. narrative, expository, poetry). A child's instructional level might be higher with narrative than it is with another type of text

Easy (Independent)	1. % of accuracy (word recognition)	= 95% or higher
	2. comprehension	= full/complete = 90–100% if questions are used to score
Instructional	1. % of accuracy	= 90% or higher
	2. comprehension	= partial, but satisfactory = 75–89% if questions are used to score
Frustrational	1. % of accuracy	= below 90%
	2. comprehension	= fragmented = less than 75% if questions are used to score

Figure 3.9 Levels Attained on the Running Record

at the same level. Report results according to the benchmarks on Figure 3.9, but add a qualifier in the comments whenever you feel that the calculations alone misrepresent the child's performance. For example, if the accuracy was 85% and comprehension was satisfactory, identify the text as borderline frustrational. From observations you've noted, cite evidence for your conclusions in a comment area on the reporting sheet. For example:

With an accuracy of 85% and satisfactory comprehension, the calculations indicate that this text is borderline frustrational level for Jake. He appears to have relied heavily on prior knowledge of the topic and failed to pick up new information presented in the passage. It wasn't totally frustrational since he got the main idea, but he needs support and guided instruction in critical reading skills. Several word substitutions seem to have created confusion with new facts and terminology in the passage. Jake effectively uses background knowledge but needs to read critically to affirm, correct, or add to his base information on a topic if he is to expand it. He agreed to listen to the tape, note his miscues, and then try repeated readings to build fluency and improve comprehension. We also talked about pacing reading, especially on informational passages. His assumption that the text will only be a repeat of known facts tends to cause inefficient reading.

ERROR-FREQUENCY RATE

The error rate score is an approximation of the number of words a child reads correctly before the flow is interrupted with a miscue.

The error frequency gives an indication of fluency and correlates with comprehension. Connections within and across sentences are richer when readers take the information in meaningful units. A high score indicates that a large number of words—constituting meaningful intake—were accurately read before the flow of language and thought was interrupted. Error frequency as a secondary indicator of fluency is discussed in Chapter 5. To obtain the error-frequency rate (E), divide the number of words in the selection by the number of errors.

> **Example:** If the text had a total of 182 words (as in the accuracy example) and the reader made 7 errors, I'd divide 182 by 7 and get 26. This shows that the reader made an error approximately every 26th word. Remember, it's not exact; it's an approximation.

SELF-CORRECTION PERCENT

The self-correction figure indicates the degree of self-monitoring and self-maintenance that a reader uses. Students who expect reading to make sense will recognize when they make errors. Those who have begun to take charge of their reading will work to fix the problem. They'll self-correct miscues that don't make sense and interrupt meaning. The goal is to increase the number of miscues that are self-corrected. Uncorrected miscues inhibit efficient comprehension. If the teacher celebrates self-correction, consistently drawing attention to it, children will increase their efforts to do it. When giving feedback on a reading session, comment on the self-corrections you observe. For example, say,

> I could tell you were thinking about what you were reading when you corrected this word. And, when you went back to reread, you fixed these errors. Good readers use fix-up strategies like this. You're doing more self-correcting than before.

To report self-correction percent (SC percent), follow this calculation: errors divided by self-corrections plus errors times 100.

$$\frac{E}{SC + E} \times 100 = SC \text{ percent}$$

> **Example**: In our example, the reader had 7 uncorrected errors and 2 self-corrections. Remember the self-corrections don't count as errors.

2/7+2 = 2/9 = 0.22 X 100 = 22% (rounded to the nearest whole)

As with E, this is an approximation. The reader corrected approximately 22% of the errors made. He corrected 2 of the 9 original errors, leaving 7 uncorrected. Thus, 2 SCs on 9 errors compute to 22% of errors corrected.

Key Concepts

Self-monitoring: the reader self-checks for accuracy and understanding as he reads.

Self-maintenance: the reader self-initiates efforts to fix errors, demonstrating knowledge of and independence in using strategies for decoding and comprehension.

USING DATA TO PLAN TEACHING POINTS

Note children's self-correction percents and plan demonstrations of strategies for self-correcting miscues when reading aloud. Verbalize your thinking to show how it's done. You can self-correct miscues immediately or reread to fix one, going back to any that confused meaning. Say,

Uh-oh, wait a minute. That didn't sound right. I must have mixed something up. I'd better reread this sentence. Oh, there it is. It says, … not …! I'll read this part over. (Read the sentence over with the corrected miscues and continue.) Now, it sounds right!

You might also draw attention to good models for self-correcting when children are reading aloud for the class. For example:

TEACHER: Kelly, without any help, you corrected two words that you first made mistakes on. How did you know they were wrong, and how did you figure them out?

KELLY: Here, it was talking about the kinds of farms. I didn't know the word at first. It looked like "day", but it had extra letters in the middle. So I just said "day". Then, I thought it had to be like a farm where we get milk because the picture had cows in the field. I thought of "dairy". I heard my Mom use that word for food with

As you observe a child during an oral reading session, answer the following questions.

Does the child:

• try to make overall sense of what she's reading?

• read smoothly so that the reading sounds like talking?

• use context (meaning or semantic) cues?

• read in meaningful phrases or chunks?

• make logical predictions about words she's uncertain of?

• use her knowledge of language patterns (syntactic cues—what kinds of words come next to sound the way we order words when we talk)?

• use confirmation and self-correction strategies?

• use the cues in an integrated (orchestrated) way?

• appear to be enjoying reading?

Figure 3.10 What to Watch for While They Read
Source Adapted from ILEA/Center for Language in Primary Education, 1989, pp. 41–42; Shea, 2000, 2006

milk in it. When I started to say it again with the /r/ in the middle part, I said "dairy".

SAMPLE RECORDS FOR PRACTICE

Practice reading and following RRs with the additional sample records at the companion website. There are scripts with the RR markings like the *Arthur Writes a Story* example in this chapter. Those have the percent of accuracy, E, and self-correction percent calculated; review the scored miscues and calculations for each. The video at the website adds another dimension, allowing assessment of the child's demeanor during the task. Body language, expressions, and gestures add information to the overall assessment. This data, often missed when busy taking a RR, can be analyzed when reviewing a recording.

YOU'RE A RECORDER NOW

You've done it! You've carefully observed readers in your class and noted strategies they use and behaviors they exhibit. You've gathered objective data and computed word-reading accuracy, error frequency, and self-correction percent. Use the questions listed in Figure 3.10 as you reflect on the overall performance.

You're noticing patterns in children's development and tailoring your teaching to these observations in efforts to meet each child's specific needs.

The next step is to analyze miscues, assess reading fluency, and evaluate the child's comprehension of what was read. Although you've been informally checking children's understanding, now is the time to formalize this part of the process. Chapter 6 discusses how to formalize this part of the process.

EXTENDING THE DISCUSSION

- Examine the RRs at the companion website, including the video recording. Follow the markings and their match to the text.
- Practice using the form for anecdotal note taking while listening to a child read. Share these recorded insights about children's reading performances at a meeting with colleagues. Discuss your insights.
- Use audio or video equipment to record children as they read aloud and retell. Work with colleagues to do a RR for each child, marking miscues according to the code. Discuss your experience.

Part III
Digging Deeper
Reading Performance Reveals Process and Product

4

ASSESSING READING ACCURACY

MISCUE ANALYSIS: USING AND MISSING THE CUES

Goodman (1973) called students' reading errors miscues since they pinpoint where the reader missed cues (clues) in the text—embedded ones that facilitate word identification when used effectively. Goodman referred to miscues as "windows on the reading process" (1982, p. 93). They're windows into students' thinking. "Miscues allow us to see the cues that readers are using effectively, those they're using, but confusing, those they're not integrating with other cues, and those they're not using at all" (Shea, 2006, p. 81). Drawing the reader's attention to miscues helps him understand where and why he went off track.

When the oral reading and retelling are completed, compliment the reader on the performance citing a specific positive behavior in the reading as well as in the retelling. Then, add comments; discuss one or two significant miscues and an aspect about the retelling. You never want to overdo teaching points at this time. Less is more. It's important to note that, although discussed separately in Chapters 3–6, the completion of calculations, miscue analyses, and recording of conclusions occurs after the entire interaction with the reader has concluded.

> ## Key Concept
>
> **Significant miscue**: word-reading error in the oral reading that changes meaning in the passage.

ANALYZING MISCUES

Later in the day, review the tape. Check the coding used, mark off one minute of reading, expand on notes taken during the retelling, and listen for indicators of fluency. Then complete calculations for accuracy, error-frequency rate, percent of self-correction, and WCPM. Now, it's time to examine individual miscues and add that information to the RR form. Do a thorough analysis of all miscues, searching for patterns in the reader's use of semantic, syntactic, and graphophonemic (letter/sound) cues. Fluency and retelling (comprehension) are discussed in Chapters 5 and 6; both will be evaluated and reported; conclusions for each are then added to the form.

A closer look at the reader's errors reveals a pattern of cue use and nonuse. Sometimes, you need to review more than one RR before patterns are discernable. That knowledge guides the goals you set with the reader and more immediate follow-up instruction.

Return to the RR form and study, line by line, substitution errors in relationship to their immediate context. Comment on other types of miscues in your reporting, but, obviously, those cannot be compared to words in the text for appropriateness across the cue categories.

Decide whether the substitution error is semantically (meaning) appropriate (i.e. a synonym). Did it impede comprehension? There may be debate about shades of differences with meaning appropriateness.

Consider the substitution's syntactic (grammatical) appropriateness. Is it the same part of speech, same verb tense, or same number (singular or plural)? Be firm about syntactic appropriateness; it needs to match across all dimensions of grammatical structure. Noticing variations in word forms is important for distinguishing exact meaning as well as spelling and writing development.

Examine the substitution for letter/sound matches with the text word. Use your best judgment, but try to not allow too much liberty.

Suppose a child needs to figure out what word comes after:

Bears live in the _____.

• Using *semantic* (meaning) cues, he can begin to figure out what the word might be. Knowing that the word can't be just any word in the world makes the task of figuring it out less daunting. You can encourage readers by saying, "Get your brain thinking of words that would make sense with the other words in the sentence."

• Using *syntactic* (grammar) cues, he is aware that a word that makes sense here would have to be a place or thing (noun). Or, it could be a word that describes a place or thing (adjective) named after this word. He realizes it couldn't be an action word (verb), because that would not sound right—the way we talk.

• Putting semantic and syntactic cues together as *context clues*, the child narrows the possibilities for what the unknown word could be and begins to make logical predictions. It might be *cage, cave, zoo, woods,* or *forest.*

• Using *visual cues*, he can test those words. Remind children, "Use your eyes to see if all the letters you'd need for one of those words are on the page in that place. Pictures are another type of visual clue."

• The child may think of *woods* but see c-a-v-e. He cannot confirm woods based on the letters he sees. *Graphophonemic cues* (letter/sound clues) cause him to try another prediction or analyze the word carefully to decode it as one he hadn't expected.

Figure 4.1 Integrating Cues for Word Solving

MEANING APPROPRIATE MISCUES

Meaning appropriate (M column) substitutions make sense and do not interrupt general comprehension of the sentence, paragraph, or passage. M appropriate miscues may or may not be syntactically appropriate (S). They may or may not have a letter/sound (L-S) correlation. Sometimes, M miscues are synonyms that enhance clarity.

For example, in the sentence, *Bears live in the _____,* the child may read *forest, wild,* or *woods* for *cave* after referring to picture clues. These would not interrupt meaning and would be syntactically appropriate. However, none of these miscues incorporate a L-S match.

Let me note here that I have a consistent way of categorizing nonwords. I automatically score nonword miscues unacceptable for meaning and syntax since I have no basis for considering a fit in those categories. I do consider their L-S similarity.

Cue System	Description
Semantic or meaning (M)	*Semantic* cues are derived from meaning—the meaning of the other words in the sentence, surrounding sentences, and whole text. Readers must be able to read and understand most of the words in a sentence to use semantic cues for decoding unknown words. When the predicted word is meaning appropriate and also fits other cue systems, chances are good it's correct (the word in the text).
Syntactic (S) or grammatical	*Syntactic* knowledge reflects one's awareness of sentence grammar. Readers use it to predict what kind of word would *fit* in the sentence. Efficient readers instantly crosscheck syntactic expectations with letter/sound cues.
Graphophonic or letter/sound (L-S)	*Graphophonic* relates to the letter (grapheme) sequences in words and their match with each speech sound (phoneme). Sometimes, more than one letter is used to represent a speech sound (e.g. *ai* for long *a*). Competent readers use letter/sound knowledge to recognize words fluidly and effortlessly. They use this knowledge interactively with other cues.

Figure 4.2 Categories of Miscues
Source Goodman, 1973, pp. 158–176; Shea, 2006, p. 82

SYNTACTICALLY APPROPRIATE MISCUES

Syntactically appropriate (S) substitutions keep sentence structure intact, although they may or may not keep meaning intact. For example, a child may read *cart* when the word is *cave*. In this case, it has a L-S match. It is a thing or place (S), but it doesn't make sense (M). The reader is applying what he knows about how the language goes together and what kind of a word belongs in this place.

Young children know that a describing or naming word (the term for the part of speech is not important at this point) would come next in the sentence, *Bears live in the* ____, because they've heard the language and use it to communicate. The child is using L-S and language structure knowledge to attempt the word. But, he's not cross-checking for meaning by applying the self-monitoring question: *Does the word I'm saying make sense in this place?* If the child was only using L-S information and not syntax, he might have said, *Bears live in the call.* If he was using all cueing systems—meaning, syntax, and L-S—he might have said *cage* (like bears in a zoo) as a miscue.

Hopefully, the child would have realized when reading on that *cage* would not be appropriate if these bears were in the wild. Good readers stop when reading has broken down and go back to reread and apply fix-up strategies. Such behavior reflects self-monitoring and a reader's demonstration of self-maintenance.

Meaning Appropriate Miscues

Miscue	Text	Error Match		
		M	S	L-S
forest	cave	Y	Y	–
wild	cave	Y	Y	–
woods	cave	Y	Y	–

Syntactically Appropriate Miscues

Miscue	Text	Error Match		
		M	S	L-S
cart	cave	–	Y	Y
call	cave	–	–	Y
cage	cave	Y	Y	Y

Graphophonemically (Letter-Sound) Appropriate Miscues

Miscue	Text	Error Match		
		M	S	L-S
home	house	Y	Y	Y
whale	wheel	–	Y	Y

Figure 4.3 Determining Appropriateness of Miscues

MISCUES WITH LETTER-SOUND SIMILARITY

L-S match substitutions refer to the similarity in letters and sounds between the miscue and the word in the text. As shown, miscues that match in L-S may or may not be meaningful or syntactically appropriate.

For example, *home* for *house* matches in L-S to some degree; this miscue is also meaning (M) and syntactically appropriate (S). However, *whale* for *wheel* isn't meaning appropriate (M) although there is a L-S match and it is the same part of speech (S).

Some L-S matches may be minimal—only a beginning or ending sound similarity, but closely resemble the size and shape of the text word (configuration). You can record B (beginning), M (middle), or E (ending) in the L-S column to designate the location of a minimal L-S match.

SIGNIFICANT AND INSIGNIFICANT MISCUES

Miscues that inhibit a child's understanding of the text and diminish fluency are considered significant. Comprehension quickly becomes fragmented when decoding lacks smoothness, automaticity, and reasonable accuracy. Miscues that do not interrupt overall understanding of the passage are insignificant. However, if a reader makes many insignificant miscues, there's a risk that he's altering or misinterpreting the author's message.

There can be considerable differences in teachers' perception of significant and insignificant miscues. That's why it's a good idea to establish a schoolwide policy; teachers often decide to count all miscues in the accuracy score—even though some informal reading inventories suggest that only significant ones are factored into an accuracy score. They note when an accuracy score is borderline (almost at the next level) because of insignificant miscues, but report the score as calculated with all miscues counted.

MISCUE PATTERNS

The analysis of one RR will not be conclusive; studying several may create a distinct pattern that reveals how the child uses, misuses, or overuses cues. Analyzing the reader's pattern of miscues can help the teacher plan instruction that reinforces developing skills, introduces new skills when readiness is apparent, and emphasizes an integrated use of the cueing systems. Just as a musical conductor knows when to bring in a section of the symphony, efficient readers employ appropriate cue systems as they navigate texts. Clay (2004) also analyzes self-corrections (corrected miscues) for semantic, syntactic, and graphophonemic appropriateness. Often, reasons for self-corrections are obvious; when they're not, ask the reader for an explanation during the follow-up discussion. You might ask, "I noticed that you self-corrected here. How did you know that ... was wrong? How did you figure out this word?" When looking for miscue patterns, keep a caveat in mind: if the text read is too hard, miscue analysis can misinform.

Miscues made in frustrational level text generally fall in the L-S category. Children trying to read text at that level cannot apply meaning and syntactic cues when they don't know most of the words. They're left with only one tool—L-S cues. Consequently, miscues made on frustrational level text should be used cautiously when searching for a pattern.

If the reader's miscues are predominately meaning and syntactically appropriate, she's focused on understanding the gist of the passage. Good readers make these kinds of miscues as they read to maintain the flow of comprehension. Encourage readers to inquire about new words in order to enlarge their reading, writing, listening, and speaking vocabularies. Explain how readers sometimes need to stop and use the book's glossary or ask about a word that labels a concept central to understanding the passage (i.e. a technical term). This is especially true with informational text.

Often, young children with extensive oral language vocabularies make miscues that improve a very simple text. They insert words and phrases that are in their speaking vocabularies, but too complex for use in an emergent level text. In such a case, a child's word reading accuracy may be low, while his comprehension is very high. If children habitually use meaning and syntax substitutions to improve simple text, it can be problematic for benchmark score purposes. When the reader's miscues change the author's message, subtly or dramatically, he may become confused, misinterpret the author's point, or draw false conclusions. Explain the importance of reading the author's words; in retelling, readers can elaborate.

SAMPLE MISCUE ANALYSIS WITH WORDS CORRECT PER MINUTE

Review the RRs introduced in Chapter 3. The record for *If You Traveled the Underground Railroad* is shown in Figure 4.5 with miscues analyzed on the form. A chart has also been created to analyze the same miscues. Some people prefer to use the chart as a history of collected miscues. It can be easier to read. Squeezing multiple analyses into boxes on the RR form, especially when there are several substitutions in the line, can get tricky. The RR examples at the companion website also show the miscue analysis for each session.

The one-minute mark is also shown on each. The WCPM score (number of words read correctly to that one-minute mark) is recorded as well. Figure 4.4 shows the guide introduced in the previous chapter—one for recording information on the RR form; note the explanation for scoring miscues. Figure 4.5 presents an example of analysis for substitution miscues on a RR form. You will also notice that the one-minute point is marked for the child's reading. The word at that point was *Christmas* on page 47, line 11—the 100th word in the passage.

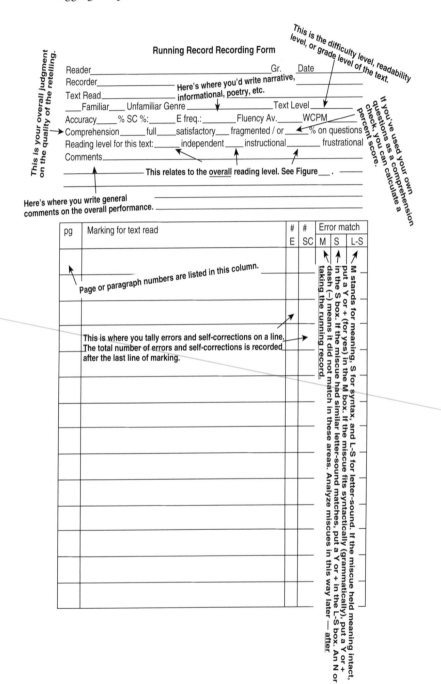

Figure 4.4 Guide for Recording Information and Scores on the Running Record Form (scoring miscues)

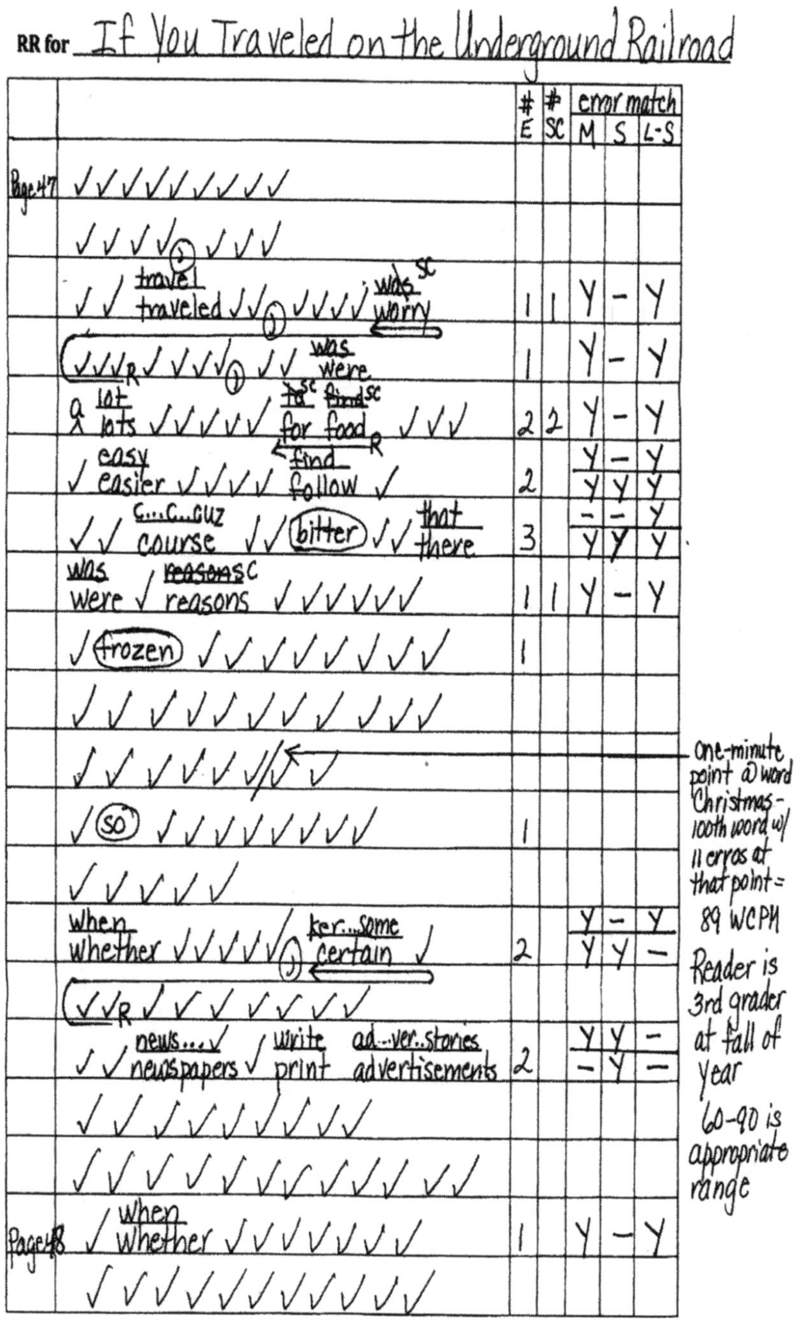

RR for _If You Traveled on the Underground Railroad_

Figure 4.5 Sample Running Record with Miscue Analysis (*Underground Railroad*)

If You Traveled on the Underground Railroad (cont.)

				#E	#SC	error match M	S	L-S
Page 48	✓ ✓ ✓ ✓ ✓ ✓ ✓ towards ~~toward~~ ✓			1		Y	Y	Y
	total			18	4			

accuracy $= 182 \div 200 = 91\%$

E freq. $= 200 \div 18 = 11 =$ an error every 11th word

SC % $= \frac{4}{18+4} \times 100 = .18 \times 100 = 18\%$

Figure 4.5 (Continued)

At that point the reader had made 11 miscues. The WCPM is calculated as 100 − 11 or 89 WCPM. (This score falls within the appropriate range (60–90) since the child was a third grader in the fall of an academic year.) The concept of WCPM and its relevance will be explored with a discussion of fluency in Chapter 5.

This reader was self-monitoring for meaning; he applied L-S knowledge. One syntactically inappropriate miscue was caused by an effort to make another miscue fit. After inserting the word *a*, the child read *lots* as a singular word—*lot*. He had difficulty discriminating the high frequency words—*was, were, that, there,* and *when.* He also dropped endings—*travel* for *traveled* and *easy* for *easier.* He used a meaningful substitution—*write* for *print (The newspapers wouldn't print).* However, the loss of specifics affected comprehension. The newspaper did print stories, but not *advertisements* for lost slaves on Sunday. Examine other types of miscues and report your conclusions in the *Comments* area on the form. How did these affect comprehension and reveal word solving strategies used by the reader? Then, begin to examine the multiple dimensions of reading fluency.

LOOKING AT FLOW

Fluency is a multi-faceted, complex, and critically important aspect of the reading act—one that's easily recognized when listening to an oral reading, but harder to measure. It needs to be objectively analyzed against the range of criteria described in the next chapter for a complete picture of a reader's current stage of fluency development. WCPM, introduced in this chapter, is one data point considered in an evaluation of fluency with a reading of text. The remaining components are discussed in Chapter 5.

EXTENDING THE DISCUSSION

- Examine the miscues scored in all of the examples provided. Do this individually or with others (colleagues or classmates). Do you agree with these scores? Where do you disagree? Why?
- Collect substitution miscues in your own classroom or classrooms in which you are observing. Make anecdotal notes when children read; record the miscue and text word missed with a sentence or two for context. Score these (M, S, L-S); work individually or with others. Discuss differences in opinions with regard to M, S, L-S appropriateness as well as whether miscues are significant or insignificant. Consider factors that may have caused the reader to make

If You Traveled on the Underground Railroad

Y = Yes—word is appropriate   – = negative—word is not appropriate

Miscue	Text	Error Match			Comments
		M	S	L-S	
travel	traveled	Y	–	Y	Verb tense change
was	were	Y	–	Y	Form for singular subject
lot	lots	Y	–	Y	Read singular to match insertion of a
easy	easier	Y	–	Y	Ending omitted—adjective degree change
find	follow	Y	Y	Y	
cuz	course	–	–	Y	Nonword—no for M, S
that	there	Y	Y	Y	
when	whether	Y	–	Y	
some	certain	Y	Y	–	
write	print	Y	Y	–	
stories	advertisements	–	Y	–	Attempted to be meaningful, but inaccurate in specifics
toward	towards	Y	Y	Y	Common speech error

The reader self-monitored for meaning; he tried to apply letter-sound knowledge. One syntactically inappropriate miscue was caused by an effort to make another miscue fit. After inserting the word *a*, the child read *lots* as a singular word—*lot*. He had difficulty discriminating many high frequency words. He also dropped endings. He used a meaningful substitution—*write* for *print (The newspapers wouldn't print)*—but the loss of specifics did affect comprehension.

Figure 4.6 Miscue Chart with Words Correctly Read Per Minute

particular miscues. Do readers in your school predominately use one or two cueing system? Do they hardly ever use a particular cueing system when stuck on a word? What does this reveal about reading instruction in the classroom or at the school?

• Collect other types of miscues in your classroom or classrooms in which you are observing. Categorize these by type and hypothesize why readers may have made each type. Work individually or with others. Which type seems the most common? Why might that be the case? What does this reveal about reading instruction in the classroom or at the school?

5

ASSESSING READING FLUENCY

FLUENCY: MULTIPLE COMPONENTS
WORKING SYNCHRONOUSLY

Reading fluency is discussed a great deal in schools today. It's also measured continuously. Such attention is warranted since it's positively correlated with comprehension. "Fluency has been shown to have a reciprocal [growth in one supports growth in the other] relationship with comprehension" (Stecker, Roser, & Martinez, 1998, p. 306).

Fluency instruction and practice should be a central part of all literacy curricula (Chard, Vaughn, & Tyler, 2002; Kuhn & Stahl, 2000). But, while school professionals understand the multi-faceted nature of fluency, the tools they use to assess it have recently focused on one dimension—speed.

While these assessments over-emphasize WCPM, strategic pacing based on text features and schema on the topic influence the reading rates of proficient readers. The calculation for WCPM is simply the number of text words read correctly in one minute.

But, the way that data is typically collected "creates *NASCAR readers—* who race through text and call off words as quickly as possible" (Shea, 2006, p. 71). These readers are typically the ones who struggle. They've been led to believe that getting to the end at warp speed will spell success. When it doesn't, they're frustrated and confused. There's a better way to determine WCPM using the RRs you've recorded. That's explained in this chapter.

Readers gradually move from a word accuracy stage toward fluency as they begin to recognize words automatically and accurately—with less decoding by sounds or parts (Schreiber, 1980). While in the word accuracy stage, beginning readers are focused on word solving—getting the words right. The result is deliberate, halting, expressionless reading. That kind of text processing interferes with the simultaneous processing of meaning (Rasinski, 2000, 2003, 2008).

You want readers to begin to understand that the goal is to make their reading sound like talking—with appropriate pacing, phrasing, expression, and intonation (Cecil, 2007a; Rasinski, 2008). When those components operate synchronously, fluency is achieved. "Fluency results from a complex interrelationship of processes that is more than the sum of these component parts" (Fountas & Pinnell, 2001, p. 316). Reading-aloud models and shared reading experiences provide a road map to that goal.

Key Concepts

Reading fluency: reading marked by a synchronous combination of word recognition accuracy, confidence, appropriate pacing, and smooth flow (i.e. characterized by appropriate expression, voice pitch, intonation, word phrasing, and word emphasis).

Read-aloud model: while reading aloud, the teacher demonstrates fluent reading as well as self-correction of miscues, musing (aloud) about meaning, and resolving confusion in understanding.

Shared reading: the teacher introduces the text and reads it aloud before guiding discussion of its content with children. Then, students are invited to reread the text chorally with the teacher before engaging in follow-up activities.

Text processing: saying the words correctly when reading.

READING ACCURACY: WORDS CORRECT PER MINUTE

Fluent reading is characterized by *flow* (smoothness) and *automaticity* (rapid recognition of words) (Flurkey, 1998, 2001; Samuels, 2002). Allington (2001) adds that automaticity requires a high level of automatic information processing as well as word processing. It involves "the ability to engage and coordinate a number of complex subskills and strategies with little cognitive effort" (p. 72).

When words are instantly recognized more cognitive energy can be directed to the other components of fluency—and to comprehension (Hudson, Lane, & Pullen, 2005). Rasinski's (2008) approximate rates for words read correctly per minute provide a benchmark for levels of automaticity. When a reader's accuracy score for oral reading is instructional on grade level text and his WCPM score is within (or near) the expected range for the grade (and time of year), he's progressing adequately on this indicator. See Figure 5.1. Another oral reading fluency table—one that reports expected WCPM scores for grades 1–8—can be found at the companion website (Hasbrouck & Tindal, 2006).

Use this performance factor cautiously and in concert with assessment of other elements of fluency and demands of the text read. WCPM alone is insufficient; it needs to be factored into the scoring on the rubric for overall fluency. See Figure 5.2.

Play back the recording of the child reading. Make a slash after the word read at the one-minute point. Count the number of words read correctly to the mark. You don't have to start timing at the first word if the reader got off to a slow start; timing the one minute can begin at any point. You can even time for two or three minutes, total the WCPM for each minute, and, then, compute the average for a final WCPM.

When calculating WCPM this way, undue stress has not been created. There's no stopwatch ticking in the tester's hand. It's done after a natural reading performance (Shea, 2006).

Compare the WCPM score you've calculated to the table below. The numbers are offered as benchmark approximations. When the child's rate falls close to the range, consider his fluency satisfactory. Rates significantly below the range indicate problems with fluency. On the other hand, substantially rapid reading is also indicative of a fluency problem (Rasinski, 2008).

Norms for WCPM in Oral Reading

Grade	Fall	Winter	Spring
1	0–20	20–40	40–60
2	40–60	50–80	70–100
3	60–90	70–100	90–120
4	90–110	100–120	110–130
5	95–115	110–130	120–140

Figure 5.1 Words Correctly Read Per Minute
Source Rasinski, 2008, as adapted from Hasbrouck and Tindal, 2006, p. 639

Possible Score/ Actual Score	Confidence	Flow/Pace of Reading	Word Reading Accuracy	Prosody/Expression
4	The reader was relaxed throughout the reading and self-corrected when meaning was lost.	Most of the reading was done in meaningful phrases. The reader's *flow* (movement across the lines of print) was strategically adjusted to the overall text, content, and decoding demands. Pacing was highly appropriate.	Word reading accuracy was high. The reader self-corrected most miscues.	The reader attended to print cues (i.e. punctuation) to effectively make changes in voice pitch, intonation, and word/phrase emphasis. The reader's use of expression reflected full comprehension.
3	The reader was relaxed most of the time, but appeared a little nervous whenever a miscue was made. He had some difficulty recovering flow.	Much of the reading was completed in meaningful phrases, but a few parts were "choppy" (inappropriate phrasing). The reader's *flow* mostly demonstrated appropriate pacing, but there were instances of awkward phrasing and pauses.	Some miscues that did not interrupt meaning were left uncorrected.	There was evidence of attention to print cues. The reader often made changes in voice pitch, intonation, and word/phrase emphasis in ways that matched the text and reflected comprehension.
2	The reader appeared somewhat nervous. He became flustered whenever a miscue was made and struggled to regain flow.	Much of the reading was completed in halting, disjointed, or word-by-word speaking The reader's *flow* was significantly affected as he tried to apply word recognition and comprehension strategies.	The reader left uncorrected errors that did interrupt meaning.	The reader attempted to make changes in voice pitch, intonation, and word/phrase emphasis based on print cues, but the overall effect was monotone. The reader tried to be expressive, but it did not match the text or reflect comprehension.
1	The reader was obviously nervous to a point that concentration on the reading was impaired.	Most or all of the reading was completed in halting (word-by-word) speech with long hesitations. The reader's *flow* was interrupted as he tried to apply word recognition and comprehension strategies.	The reader frequently made and left uncorrected errors that did interrupt meaning.	The reading was done in a monotone voice with little attention to print cues. There were no attempts to add emphasis, adjust pitch and intonation, or use expression.
score in each column →				

Student's average fluency score = _____ (add scores for each column and divide by 4)

Figure 5.2 Rubric for Evaluating Fluency
Sources Fountas and Pinnell, 2006; Fountas and Pinnell, 2001, 2005; Academic Standards and Resources: *Fluency Rubric*, retrieved June 14, 2005 from http://www.indianastandardsresource. org/documents/1.pdf; Shea, 2006

CONFIDENCE

The reader's level of confidence is the first factor assessed on the rubric. The belief in one's ability to successfully complete a task significantly affects motivation, persistence, and performance. NASCAR readers are propelled by stress—an implicit or self-imposed demand to beat the stopwatch or a previous score.

It's difficult to be confident that you'll recognize and be able to say words quickly in that circumstance. In a rush to the finish line, NASCAR readers are less likely to take time to self-correct miscues if they do trip on words. The reader who self-corrects knows that accuracy, meaning, and flow act reciprocally. Each supports the others.

FLOW

Flurkey (1998) compared effective reading to a smoothly moving river. A lazy river becomes stagnant; things get caught up, decay, and the waters become murky. Raging rivers overrun their banks, causing devastating results. Neither is working in harmony with nature. But, a smoothly flowing river adjusts its pace to the surroundings; it slows down at a bend and picks up speed on a straightaway to the sea.

Teachers look for that third kind of river flow in children's reading. "Flow is about pacing or rate variability that's just right [for the particular text]; it's about smoothness of movement" (Shea, 2006, p. 72). Fluent readers flow through text as they read; they recognize most words automatically and can decode new ones with minimal effort. They're in harmony with the author as they link words meaningfully and think about the message.

PHRASING

Reading words in appropriate phrases is critically important for understanding text. Meaning doesn't reside in isolated words, but in the appropriate linking of them into meaningful phrases (Rasinski, 2003).

Good phrasing enhances word and error recognition. The reverse is also true; automatic and accurate reading facilitates natural word chunking into meaningful strings. The ability to link words together is strengthened when word recognition is automatic and accurate (Shea, 2006). Fluent readers connect words into meaningful phrases "as they read, capturing key ideas and connections" (Shea, 2006, p. 74); they comprehend the message. See Figure 5.3. Appropriate phrasing

Read this sentence word by word.

> The … little … girl … happily … skipped … along … the … path.

It's difficult to grasp meaning. You're anxiously waiting for each next word, hoping that it'll help you make sense. It's like a game of charades—working with small units—word by word—trying to predict the whole.

Try reading the sentence with an attempt to link words.

> The little … girl … happily … skipped along … the path.

Understanding is still an effort. You're trying to merge semi-chunked bits together as you proceed. That's extra and needless cognitive effort before overall meaning can be achieved.

Now read it chunked this way …

> The little girl/happily skipped/along the path.

Try it with an extension. There's more to get in one breath, but it sounds natural when we read the longer chunk as one unit.

> The little girl/happily skipped/along the path to her Grandma's house.

When the words are recognized effortlessly and read accurately in meaningful units like this, understanding is seamless.

Figure 5.3 Chunking Words into Meaningful Phrases
Source Adapted from Shea, 2006, p. 75

leads to another aspect of fluency—one that reveals personal interpretations; this is prosody.

PROSODY

Fluent reading is *prosodic*. Prosody is "a linguistic concept that refers to such features in oral reading as intonation, pitch, stress, pauses, and the duration placed on specific syllables" (Vacca, Vacca, Gove, Burkey, Lenhart, & McKeon, 2003, p. 214). When reading reflects such qualities you can just about hear the mind wheels turning and mental gears humming. "It is clear that the amount of correct expression indicates to the trained ear how much the reader comprehends the text" (Hudson et al., 2005, p. 705). It's expression that sounds natural—like talking; it's not affected or extreme. I don't expect to hear a rehearsal for a drama queen!

Good speakers are models of prosody. They hold your attention when they synchronize the elements of prosody in artful ways. It's easy to follow and understand the message. Resonant voicing holds attention and guides listeners toward key points. Prosody practice has benefits for silent reading too.

PROSODY IN SILENT READING

Fluent oral reading has a notable impact on silent reading. Proficient silent readers hear their inner prosodic voice when interacting with text (Pinnell, Pikulski, Wixon, Cambell, Gough, and Beatty, 1995).

An analysis of results on a silent reading comprehension section of the National Assessment of Education Progress (NAEP) and the same students' scores on a fluency rubric indicate a strong positive correlation between the two measures (Pinnell et al., 1995). Such evidence compels us to prioritize the development of all aspects of fluency. To reach that objective, teachers constantly gather data on readers' performance in each area of fluency and use that information to plan instruction and opportunities for practice.

ASSESSING OVERALL FLUENCY

Systematic observation and documentation of reading behaviors aligned with all sections of the fluency rubric are essential before draw-ing and reporting conclusions (Hudson et al., 2005). The tool teachers use to assess fluency needs to be valid; it must measure genuine ele-ments of real fluency (Rasinski, 2008). Teachers need to determine whether the assessment tool gathers information on every dimension of fluency—and whether there's any instructional *utility* (usefulness) for the data captured. They should ask, "Can it meaningfully inform my instruction?" The rubric in Figure 5.2 includes all the ingredients of fluency. It can be used it to assess students' current level in each area. That information enables teachers to plan instruction that coaches readers to the next level. But, there are steps to take before using the rubric.

Effective teachers demonstrate fluent reading repeatedly whenever they're reading aloud. Sometimes, they ask students to collabora-tively score these demonstrations using the rubric. As a group, the teacher and class discuss the children's scoring. Allington (1983) emphasizes that teacher modeling is critically important since texts only provide subtle clues (i.e. punctuation) to direct prosodic reading. "Many [readers] need to see how the expert reader decides when to use prosodic elements when signals are missing" (Shea, 2006, p. 77).

Next, teachers have students read to each other; peers score, share, and discuss rationale for scores they've recorded. The activity builds confidence and competence; it makes readers continuously aware of meaningful fluency indicators. After these experiences, teachers assess students individually through the RR; then add their fluency scores (fluency rubric average and WCPM) to the RR form. Taken together, this information reveals "a great deal about his [the reader's] ability to successfully navigate the text I've asked him to read" (Shea, 2006, p. 79).

When scores indicate that the reader is dysfluent, pinpoint the difficulty and ameliorate it quickly. Sometimes, however, you need to dig deeper—when markers lead to a certain aspect of fluency. For example, if word reading accuracy is low, you need to examine the reader's miscues and build decoding skills associated with the cueing systems the reader is not using effectively. If comprehension is weak, consider how the flow of text processing is interrupting the reader's understanding.

THE NEXT STEP

A full RR involves retelling. Without that, teachers only have a measure of *text processing* with limited indication of understanding (e.g. with use of appropriate expression). Retelling measures the reader's self-initiated and expanded *meaning processing*. Teacher prepared or companion scripted questions control comprehension, leading readers to wait until they're quizzed before thinking about the text, assume that only what's asked is important, or become passive about interacting with text content. Scripted questions direct readers' attention, limiting personal construction of connections and expression of understanding. The goal is to encourage active, engaged reading. This creates readers who can and want to talk about text; they discuss their ideas and expect feedback from others.

When the child finishes reading, compliment his effort. Make one specific comment like, "You self-corrected miscues that didn't make sense. Good job." Then, initiate the retelling—without delay. Pausing too long to discuss the oral reading can distract a reader's attention from the content. Chapter 6 outlines procedures for measuring retelling.

Key Concept

Meaning processing: understanding the meaning; comprehending the text.

EXTENDING THE DISCUSSION

- Revisit the RRs at the companion website to review the WCPM for each record. How do the scores for these readers compare to scores expected for the grade? How and where did miscues interrupt flow in these records?
- Discuss the criteria in the rubric for evaluating fluency. Why are these aspects important? How does each contribute to the whole—smooth, accurate reading that enables comprehension? What would you add? Explain why.
- Record children reading aloud. Working with colleagues, determine their WCPM at different points in the reading. Evaluate the fluency of each child's reading across all areas of the rubric.

6

ASSESSING READING COMPREHENSION

RETELLING: MORE THAN SUMMARIZING

You've practiced recording children's oral reading, marking miscues and the WCPM in order to assess fluency in word recognition. This is the first part of a complete RR.

Although smooth reading is essential for efficient comprehension, it doesn't guarantee it. It's possible for a child to say the words with a high degree of accuracy without processing any meaning. Most teachers have worked with children who do this. Therefore, the child's understanding of what he reads needs to be assessed separately from his word reading accuracy with decoding the words. Without meaning, the activity is not reading—it's word calling.

A process for systematically assessing children's comprehension of what they've read through their self-initiated expression of the understanding they've constructed is called *retelling*. Retelling is more than summarizing. In a summary, the reader rephrases the gist of the text with a modicum of inference—or none at all. On the other hand, retellings are "supersized, *summary-plus* responses." They "reveal the range, depth, and personal nature of their [readers'] understanding; retellings resemble in-the-world literate interactions" (Shea, 2006, p. 38)

The teacher asks the child to retell what she has just read. Although this chapter focuses on using retelling to complete a full RR (oral reading and comprehension assessment), retelling can also be used after silent independent reading (e.g. during DEAR time) or during guided reading sessions. You might ask a child to retell the content of a teacher read-aloud to assess listening comprehension. Whenever they're used, retellings are a highly effective strategy for assessing a reader's overall comprehension of a text.

Key Concept

Guided reading: session for small group reading instruction focused on students' common needs, readiness, or interest using text at their instructional level. After teacher-led pre-reading activities, children read independently. The teacher guides follow-up discussion, scaffolding students' comprehension of the text.

WHY USE RETELLING?

Retellings are a valuable assessment tool. In a retelling, readers:

- demonstrate what they remember about the main ideas and the details of the text;
- integrate personal interpretations and connections;
- learn to self-monitor their comprehension in a structured way as they internalize the process;
- come to understand that reading requires critical thinking, understanding, and the construction of meaning with text. They realize that merely saying words is not enough;
- anticipate having to retell and consequently become more engaged with the text, more sensitive to the possibility of varied interpretations, and more aware of text structures;
- become active readers projecting themselves into a text—to view story events, relationships, or facts as a participant rather than as an observer;
- develop expressive oral language skills, building fluency and confidence in oral presentations of personal ideas;
- develop more sophisticated language structures for relating their own stories and anecdotes.

MAKING RETELLING USEFUL

With a consistent way of assessing students' retelling, you'll have reliable data for planning effective instruction. It also documents growth in students' comprehension.

Standardize retellings by using checklists as children retell what they've read. When children are familiar with graphic organizers for narrative and expository text, their retellings follow the format outlined by them. The organizer also creates a mental model for attending to and thinking about information while reading. It's helpful to post organizers in the classroom, providing children a reference when reading or retelling.

TEACHING RETELLING

Help students understand that the order, content, and sequence of a retelling are based on the kind of writing (genre) that was read. Talk about the guidelines for telling someone all about what you've read. See Figure 6.1.

Teachers often review various graphic organizers after teaching structures for different types of texts (i.e. narrative story grammar and expository frames—description, cause/effect, sequence). See Figures 6.2 and 6.3. It's important to make sure that students have lots of collaborative practice with the organizers and time to try them out with peers. Gradually children internalize the models for thinking on different levels when interacting with text; they begin to own the process.

1. **Decide what kind of selection (genre or kind of writing) you read.**
   Identify the genre for the text you read. Then, begin with an introduction.
   _____(name of the text read) by _____ is all about _____.

2. **If it is a story (narrative), use a narrative organizer to guide your retelling.**
   As you talk and retell, follow the organizer and tell about each topic. If you only read part of a story, pass over anything on the list that does not apply to what you read. For example, if the solution hasn't been revealed yet, you cannot talk about that.

3. **If it's an informational (expository) text, decide which main structure (frame) it follows.**
   Use the organizer that matches that structure as you retell. Sometimes the selectio uses more than one type of structure. For example, there may be a description before a problem was identified and a solution offered by the author. In that case follow more than one organizer as you retell each part of the text read.

4. **Don't forget to add your own ideas, interpretations, and connections to experiences or other books read. This makes it a summary PLUS.**
   Tell how you feel about the story or information. Was it exciting or interesting?
   Tell how this story or information is like or different from what you knew before.
   Tell if you think the author wrote in a way that is interesting and easy to understand.
   Tell if you think the story is realistic or the information is accurate.

Figure 6.1 Guidelines for Telling Someone All about What You Read

Name _____Date _____

Story_____

Characters: (Who)

Setting: (Where and When)

Problem:

Events: (Beginning, Middle, and End)

Solution: (Resolution of the Problem)

Reactions/Comments:

Figure 6.2 Organizer for Narrative Stories

The teacher introduces and explains the scoring checklists she'll be using for assessing children's retelling. The checklists are well correlated with graphic organizers children have been using. Start by modeling retelling. When you think you're finished with a demonstration, show students how you ask yourself questions (i.e. ones related to narrative story grammar or expository text frames, depending on the kind of text read) to check whether there's an area you've missed. (These questions are available at the companion website.) Ask some of the following:

- If it's a story, did I tell all the story parts? *Somebody* (character), *Where* (setting—place), *When* (setting—time), *Wanted* (problem), *But* (order of events), *So* (solution). Did I tell what I think, how it's like another book or what happened to me?
- If it's only part of the story, did I tell how it connects to what already happened? Tell everything about this part? Tell my ideas

Structure	Characteristics	Organizer
Descriptive	Presents information on a particular topic or gives characteristics of it.	Semantic Map/Web Main Idea/Topic (center) 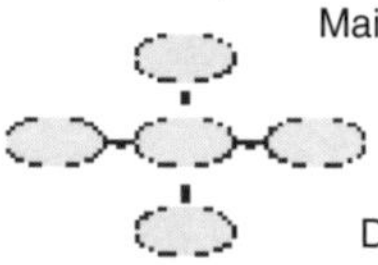 Details (outer ovals)
Collection	Presents a number of ideas or descriptions. How they relate is the focus. The order is unimportant.	List Organizer 1. 2. 3. 4.
Sequence	Presents a number of ideas or descriptions in a prescribed sequence. The order of items is key.	List Organizer or Time Line 1. 2. 3. 4.
Causation	Presents ideas in a causal relationship.	Situation/Cause and Effect Causes or reasons / Situation / Effects or results
Comparison	Presents similarities and differences between 2 or more items/ideas	Venn Diagram 1st idea only 2nd idea only both 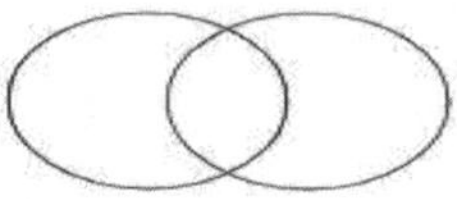
Theory/Proof	Presents a problem or theory with the author's solution or evidence.	T-Proof Organizer Opinion / Proof

Figure 6.3 Organizers for Informational Text

about what happened or the writing in this part? Tell what I think will happen next? Tell how it's like another book or what happened to me?

- If it's about comparing, did I tell how they are alike and how they are different?

- If it's a collection, did I name all of them?
- If it must be a certain way, did I tell the steps in order?
- If the author gave an opinion, did I say what it was and tell his/her reasons?
- If it described something, did I tell what it was and give important details?
- If it tells a cause for something, did I explain that and what happened because of it (effects)?
- Did I tell what I think?

Together, the teacher and students analyze the demonstrated retell and determine whether essential points on the checklist were covered.

Key Concepts

Narrative story grammar: includes elements typically associated with the structure and sequence of a story, including aspects related to characters, setting, problem, events, and resolution.

Expository text frame: a structure within expository text for organizing information. Examples include descriptive, compare and contrast, theory/proof, sequence, collection, or cause and effect frames.

Graphic organizer: visual organization of information in note and/or graphic form that stimulates recall, reconstruction of ideas, and/or recognition of connections.

PRACTICING RETELLING

Children are now ready to give it a try. Invite them to practice with a partner, using the graphic organizers and questions as a guide. Children can evaluate each other's performances; this helps them focus on what's needed for a successful retelling. Sufficient practice may take a few weeks, but it's well worth the time. After lots of rehearsal, children meet with the teacher to read one-on-one and retell.

ASSESSING THE RETELLING

Before the reading begins, it's a good idea to always remind children that they'll be expected to retell the content of what they read.

You might say, "When you finish reading, I'll ask you to tell me all about it as if I was someone who had never heard it before."

Explain exactly what you'll be doing as they talk.

> I'll be writing notes on my checklist while you talk. Then, I'll add more notes when you tell more after I ask questions. Tell as much as you can on your own. I might not have any questions to ask if you tell me everything.

The retelling checklists are meant to be flexible. As noted, if only part of the story was read, the child tells the parts that were revealed. It's important to note that not all areas on the checklist for informational text will be applicable to every text. If that's the case, write N/A (not applicable) for that item.

Children now understand what's expected since they've been taught how to retell and have had multiple opportunities to practice. They've evaluated the teacher's retelling and that of a partner. At this point, the teacher can be confident that children's performances will validly reflect current abilities. Confusion about the task or stress should not be confounding factors.

GUIDING AND RECORDING THE RETELLING

When the child has finished the oral reading (or silent reading), ask her to think about what she just read for a minute. When she's ready, she begins to retell. Listen carefully—without comments or questions—as the child retells the content and shares comments, reactions, and interpretations. Record what is told in this self-initiated part under the *Unassisted* column. See Figures 6.4 and 6.5. There are additional checklists at the companion website.

This is the hard part. The teacher needs to keep quiet! Jumping in too soon is common; teachers are tempted to offer assistance the minute a child pauses. Readers need think time. Silence in that pause stimulates more talking by the reader. If it begins to appear that the child will not continue on her own, ask, "Anything else?" to let her know she can tell more. Record her additions in the *Unassisted* column as well since this initial prompt doesn't specifically direct her attention. Continue with that prompt, until the reader indicates that she's told all she can.

At that point, check for areas of the checklist that were not addressed in her *Unassisted* retell. Ask questions directed at each of those areas. Record the child's response in the *Assisted* column. The reader could talk about that area, but needed to be prompted with a question.

Name _____ Date_____

Text __ *Shadows Are About*_____familiar

__X__unfamiliar Background information __X_full _____limited

	Unassisted Retelling	Assisted Retelling	Look Backs Needed
Named main characters	*boy and girl*		
Named other characters		*dog and cat*	
Identified setting (time/place)	*at their house*	*outside in the car, riding a bike*	
Stated initiating event	*wake up and see shadows*		
Identified problem	*Kids are telling about shadows.*		
Described attempts to solve the problem	*They find shadows and make some.*		
Identified reaction of main character to attempts and solution of problem	*N/A*		
Retold story in correct order			*Needed to look back, but sequence not critical.*
Made inferences related to the text	*It's a brother and sister. They're reading in bed.*		
Made connections with other texts or experience	*I raced my shadow on my bike.*	*My dad can make shadow animals.*	
Made evaluative statements about the writing, illustrations, or story		*I like the pictures best. They make the kids friendly. I like the rabbit.*	

Comprehension_____ full and detailed __X__partial, but satisfactory _____fragmented

Comments: *Knows a lot about shadows—relying on prior knowledge.*

Figure 6.4 Retelling Checklist for Narrative Text

Name _____ Date _____

Selection____*If You Traveled on the Underground Railroad*_____

	Unassisted Retelling	Assisted Retelling	Look Backs
Restated the main idea	*It's about when is best time for slaves to escape.*		
Restated subtopics	*It talks about why winter and summer are good.*		
Identified key terms and vocabulary			
Identified key people	*the slaves*	*hunters, slave hunters, owners of slaves*	
Made inferences	*I think summer is best.*	*Owners didn't like to chase them in winter.*	
Recognized cause and effect		*If snow covers trails, you can get lost.*	
Comprehended sequence	*Tells why summer was good, then why winter was. Then, when it would be in the newspaper.*		
Appreciated importance of content	*If you were a slave, you could die or get caught.*		
Referred to/interprets visuals	*N/A*		
Drew conclusions based on schema and information in text		*They were brave and wanted freedom. I'd be afraid, but I'd want freedom.*	

Comprehension_____full and detailed___X__partial, but satisfactory_____fragmented

Comments: *Understood overall gist—vague or confused on details.*

Figure 6.5 Retelling Checklist for Expository Text

As noted, if an item on the checklist doesn't apply to the text read, write N/A in that place. Sometimes readers need to revisit the text to reread and review illustrations. Teachers note where and when this was necessary.

Have questions in mind in case it's necessary to prompt for assisted retelling. You want to carefully word prompts so they don't, in themselves, provide information (Goodman & Burke, 1972). Keeping the questions general—not mentioning specifics—encourages the reader to develop her own insights and interpretations. See Figure 6.6.

Questions to Ask about Stories

Characters:	Who is the main character? Other characters?
	Who else was in the story? Tell me more about them.
	What was _____ like?
Setting:	Where/When did the story take place?
Plot:	Can you think of anything else that happened?
	Why did _____ happen? (Use only those events mentioned by the teller.)
	What was the problem to be solved?
Theme:	What do you think the story was telling you?
	Why do you think the author wanted to write the story?
	Do you know any other stories that try to tell you the same thing?
	(Goodman & Burke, 1972)

Questions to Ask about Informational Text

Cause/Effect:	Why did _____ happen? What happened after _____?
Proposition/Support:	What did _____ suggest? Why did _____ think _____?
Description:	What did _____ tell us about _____?
Compare/Contrast:	How are _____ and _____ alike? How are _____ and _____ different?
Collection/Sequence:	Can you talk about all the points given? Can you tell the order for the information given?

Figure 6.6 Questions to Ask about Stories and Informational Text

Many teachers encourage children to prompt a partner in the same way. It's fun to listen in when they do it while practicing. You'll pick up some techniques that way! And, it also improves the "tutor's" retelling. Children are heard using the teacher's words when giving feedback to a partner. And, they're amazingly right on target with comments. Peers also feed forward, nudging a classmate to try something new—just as the teacher tried to encourage them.

FEEDBACK, FEED FORWARD

Feedback responds with evaluative comments after a completed performance or behavior. It lets the learner know what went well and where adjustments are needed for improvement. *Feeding forward* refers to the gentle nudging or scaffolding that's provided for a learner before or during the performance; these comments are meant to encourage a more advanced performance. They help the learner appreciate his readiness for advanced behavior; he can do it. It's important to provide just enough, but not too much of each after the reading and retelling have been done (Cole, 2004).

Following the retelling, share results on the whole performance with the reader, continually emphasizing the importance of efficient word recognition *and* full comprehension. You can share notes you've taken on the reading and the checklist for retelling. It's important to always start with compliments; then, add one or two comments that are intended to move the reader toward a new goal. Here's how it might go.

TEACHER: You read a lot of words correctly. Right here you said, "The children ran to the slide in the playground. They like to slide so high that they seem to touch the sky." I'll bet you were thinking what you'd run toward. But, then you stopped and went back to reread. You read, "The children ran to the swings in the playground. They like to swing so high that they seem to touch the sky." That was a good self-correction. It shows you were thinking about what you read. How did you know you needed to fix up that part?

CHILD: When I heard myself say, "They like to slide so high that they seem to touch the sky," I knew it wasn't right because you don't slide so high—you slide down after you climb the stairs to the slide. I looked at the word again and it had *i-n-g*. I knew it was *swing* because of that and because you can *swing* up high.

T: You also talked about how they were feeling that day when the new playground was finished. I agree with you. They were proud of it because they helped build it. They'll want to keep it nice.

You described the characters, the setting—where and when—the problem the kids had with the bully, and the way they solved it.

C: They weren't afraid. They didn't do bad things, but they made him feel silly for treating people that way.

T: When you reread this, you can tell me how they made a plan to teach the bully a lesson. Next time, try to think about the order of things that happen in a story—all the important events that happened to solve the problem.

Recognizing the child's use of fix-up strategies increases the chances that he'll persist in applying them. Effective teachers make one or two teaching points about errors in each reading—trying to refrain from overkill! There'll be opportunities to discuss other points after other readings or in a group mini lesson. Patterns that emerge through the miscue, fluency, and retelling analyses suggest topics for lessons that are more likely to capture the teachable moment, presenting skills when children are ready to understand them.

TEACHER: You retold a lot of details about the characters and setting in this story. I thought you had ideas about why they needed to find the ice-cream seller. When I asked you, you told me you knew she was probably a witness. That's good mystery thinking! Share your own thoughts and opinions in the retelling. Good readers are always thinking ahead and predicting. I like to hear what clues struck you. You don't have to wait for questions.

CHILD: She was around the whole time so I think she has to know something even though she's not telling.

T: We'll see if you're right. Here you read, *Billy found the girl who was selling ice cream.* You misread this word, *girl.* Your word made sense and it sounded right, but does the author's word have the letters you'd expect to find in the word *girl*?

C: No, but I don't know that word. The picture looks like a grown-up; it's not a kid—a girl. It's not *woman* either. That would need a *w* at the beginning.

T: Putting in a word that means about the same as the word you're unsure of is a good strategy that helps you keep going and understand what you've read. Now, we can look back and talk about the word. You can learn a new word. The author's word starts with /l/ and it has a pattern like the word, *shady.* The *a* makes the long sound—/a/ and the *y* sounds like long *e*—/e/. A *y* at the end of longer words does that; it says /e/. We can drop the /sh/ in *shady*; what's left is /ady/. Now, add /l/ to the beginning and you have /l/ /ady/—*lady.* Have you ever heard the word *lady* used by anyone?

c: My mom said a lady came to the door to collect for the food drive. She was a woman.

t: A lady is a grown-up, female person. Someone might use the word woman when talking about a lady. Your word didn't seem to keep you from understanding what you read, but changing the author's words can sometimes make an important difference and lead to confusion. In this mystery, knowing that the ice-cream seller is a grown-up lady and not a child might be important.

t: In the next part, we'll see if knowing the word lady affects your predictions. When you retell again, include your own thinking—on your own—so I don't have to ask you questions about your ideas.

End the debriefing with positive, genuine closing comments.

TEACHER: Thank you for reading with me. You really showed how you're thinking as you read and using fix-up strategies when things don't make sense. You retold a lot about the story—in the order it happened. Your ideas about why Billy's friends were annoyed with him were interesting. You made a connection to something that happened to you.

What will you be working on now when you go back to your group? Will you ask Karen to see me? I think I have time to listen to another reader today.

Your stance (point of view) as a teacher is that of a neutral, interested observer—just as you'd be if you were listening to a child who runs up and excitedly tells you about something he's just read or a movie he's seen. The objective is to establish a situation where the teller can comfortably share a full and accurate performance that reflects his current level of competence.

Key Concepts

Fix-up strategies: approaches a reader uses to correct miscues and confusion related to meaning.

Teachable moment: moment in an instructional interaction when the learner is primed (i.e. prepared, ready) to learn a new skill or understand new information.

Debriefing: discussion that follows a performance or event for the purpose of reviewing information obtained from it.

COMPLETING THE RETELLING CHECKLIST

Share your final notes with the reader and use them to set goals for his next retelling. These may include: retell more on your own (as in the previous example), add more details, or tell what you think of the author's ideas. A review of the teacher's comments and boxes filled in clearly show the child areas he needs to practice and whether the book was easy, just right, or hard.

Teachers easily identify specific comprehension skills that readers are struggling with or attempting to use (e.g. inference, summarizing) as they review checklists. Common needs become evident and establish a purpose for small group strategy lessons. Perhaps, children aren't integrating or making connections with prior knowledge. Others may not be assimilating new vocabulary or key terms that the author has defined for them.

Checks alone etch a skeletal picture of the retelling. The analysis and description of the reader's performance will be richer when the checklist is replete with details. If you taped the session, you can review the recording to augment and clarify information recorded during the retelling. Teachers try to do this as soon as possible—while the episode is fresh in their mind. They fill in additional notations and reflections and make sure their handwriting is legible. It's important to clarify any shorthand that could be confusing when overly abbreviated.

When you've completed the items on the retelling checklist, ask yourself the following questions to determine whether the text was appropriate for the reader. You can use your answers to conclude a level for comprehension. See Figure 6.4 and 6.5.

QUESTION: Was the retelling full and detailed (independent level)?

ANSWER: Most of the retelling was unassisted, correct, and included comments that reflected personal connections. Therefore, it appears to be at his independent level.

Q: Was it partial, but satisfactory (instructional level)?

A: About half or several parts of the retelling needed to be prompted. Several accurate details were added only when questioning was done. The child needed to be guided in comprehending this selection or in the expression of his understanding. It is at his instructional level.

Q: Or, was it fragmented (frustrational level)?

A: He had a difficult time retelling what was read. Much was left out or confused. Important points were missed. It appears that this selection was too hard or at his frustrational level.

Key Concept

Assimilating: taking in (absorbing) new information or meaning from vocabulary or text as a whole.

TIMETABLE FOR RETELLING

Start with assessing retelling separately before adding it to the oral reading assessment. It can be after a read aloud or follow time for silent reading. Meet with one or two children a day while other children are engaging in independent activities. You'll be able to complete a retelling for everyone in the class in about two to three weeks. Of course that follows time spent introducing the process, modeling the procedures, and allowing practice with peers as described.

At this point, you're ready to put the oral reading and retelling together for a complete RR. Use the marking system to record a child's oral reading of a selection. Listen to the retelling and make notes on the checklist. See Figure 6.7. Finish the calculations and analyses. Finally, determine the overall conclusion level of the text for the reader using the split-level guide (Leslie & Caldwell, 2011). See Figure 6.8 that includes these split levels.

SPLIT LEVELS OF PERFORMANCE

When the reader's performance score for oral reading and retelling do not both fall in the same range, teachers use the split-level guide to determine the overall level of the selection for this child. Follow the arrows on Figure 6.8. Notice that comprehension is weighted heavily.

If the child's oral reading was in the independent range (95–100%), but retelling was frustrational (fragmented), the selection was overall frustrational for the reader. He could say the words, but didn't understand the message.

As well as differences in decoding and comprehension efficiency, students' performances reflect competency differences across genre types and modes of reading (i.e. oral or silent reading). Prior, Fenwick, Saunders, Ouellette, O'Quinn, & Harvey (2011) report "a clear trend emerged whereby an oral reading advantage [over silent reading] for comprehension was found for students in first through fifth graders"

- **Remind the child of the purpose for this activity**. Let him know that you want to observe how he reads and understands what was read. Explain that comprehension is essential. You want to see how he uses strategies to figure out words he doesn't know, thinks along while reading to recognize when something doesn't make sense, and uses appropriate fix-up strategies to correct miscues that interrupt comprehension. Briefly review efficient decoding strategies (i.e. CLUNK steps in Figure 3.1).

- **Start with a brief introduction of the book or section the child will read**. If the book is unfamiliar to the reader, talk about the title, cover, author, and illustrations. This will stimulate predictions about content. If the text is one the child has read before or is in the process of reading (e.g. a chapter book), have him recall the central theme or summarize what he has already read.

- **Remind the child that you'll ask for a retell when he's finished reading**. Explain that you want to know whether he can explain what it was mostly about as well as his ideas on the content. Briefly review what a good retelling includes using the items on retelling checklists.

- **Indicate where the child should start reading; then, record as he reads.** If the text is brief, allow the child to read the whole selection. Allowing the child to read beyond a minimum number of words (i.e. 100 words) is advised. The reader gains a stronger sense of the author's style and purpose; reading accuracy and comprehension improve as the reader "gets into" the text. For a chapter book or longer picture book, have a logical stopping place in mind. Let the reader know that you'll be telling him when to stop, but don't say where in advance. Indicating the stopping point before the reading starts tends to make readers rush to that place.

- **When the child finishes reading, thank him, give one compliment, and ask for the retelling.** "You didn't rush. I like the expression you used. It was just right. Now tell me all about what you just read. Pretend that I didn't just hear you read and you want me to know all about this book." As the child retells, record your observations on the appropriate retelling checklist.

- **Share highlights of the reading and retelling. Set goals collaboratively.** "I noticed that you repeated here and there. When you reread, you corrected some errors that were causing confusion. I'm so glad that you're thinking along as you read and doing something to get back on track when you notice it doesn't make sense. That's what good readers do. This word, right here, is a word that you missed several times. I'll read the sentence out loud; see if that helps you think what the word might be. I'm sure you've heard the word and even used it yourself."

    If the child still cannot identify the word, say it for him and explain its meaning. If the child identifies the word, ask him how he recognized it this time. In either case, follow up with: "What do you notice about the word that will help you remember it next time?"

    Continue with comments related to the retelling and look forward to the next session. "The only things I had to remind you about in the retelling were the setting and connections you made. You told most of the events in the order they happened. Let's talk about what you can practice before our next running record."

- **Let the child know you enjoyed your time with him.** Be sure he clearly understands what to do when he gets back to his desk. "I can see how much you've grown and that you're using strategies comfortably now. Fixing up errors seemed harder for you before. I can tell you're thinking about the content of the book as you go. Reviewing the retelling chart and practicing with a buddy is a good goal. When you get back to your desk, you can read by yourself."

Figure 6.7 Guidelines for Taking a Complete Running Record

Word Reading Accuracy (oral reading %)	Comprehension (based on retelling checklist score) Independent = full and complete Instructional = partial, but satisfactory Frustrational = fragmented	Overall level
Independent ------→	Independent -------→	Independent
Independent ------→	Instructional ------- →	Instructional
Independent ------→	Frustrational ------- →	Frustrational
Instructional ------ →	Independent -------→	Instructional
Instructional ------ →	Instructional ------- →	Instructional
Instructional ------ →	Frustrational ------- →	Frustrational
Frustrational ------ →	Independent -------→	Instructional
Frustrational ------ →	Instructional ------- →	Frustrational
Frustrational ------ →	Frustrational ------- →	Frustrational

Figure 6.8 Split Levels of Performance
Source Adapted from Leslie and Caldwell, 2011, p. 58; Shea, 2006, p. 66

(p. 189). Their research indicated that neither reading mode had an advantage for comprehension during the transitional stage at 6th grade—a point when students are typically expected to complete most reading silently. However by 7th grade, silent reading appeared to be the stronger mode for efficient comprehension. Nevertheless, it's still important to introduce and guide children's practice with silent reading in primary and elementary grades even though the effects on comprehension are not immediately apparent. A Vygotskian perspective would suggest that such practice stimulates an internal developmental process that takes time to form and come under the reader's control. "The lag in showing a positive effect on comprehension should not be taken as evidence of the lack of importance of silent reading activities at lower grade levels" (Prior et al., 2011, p. 190). However, it is important to be aware of this developmental pattern when evaluating children's reading comprehension.

Therefore, young children's comprehension scores may likely be lower when retelling text read silently. Children who are transitioning to silent reading or already do most of their reading silently may be less accurate in an oral performance even though they comprehend the content. Some readers—at any age—just get nervous when reading aloud; they perform better on silent reading and retelling.

Readers with a lot of background knowledge on a selection may overrely on what they know to support comprehension and pay less attention to the details in the selection. When this happens, they miss new information or information that contradicts their prior knowledge. Some children can read more difficult narrative texts, but have trouble with informational texts, especially ones for which they have little background knowledge.

FACTORS AFFECTING PERFORMANCE

Many variables influence overall performance. Scores are greatly affected by the child's motivation to read a particular text, background knowledge of the content, level of task persistence, and the text's genre (narrative vs. expository).

It's important to compare a child's reading across several RRs as well as other evidence of literacy growth before making overall determinations about growth. Summative evaluations should incorporate information from multiple situations. Other possible data sources include journal entries and responses in literature discussions.

Minimally, documented information from three situations in which the child used a particular skill (i.e. comprehension) should be included since each made different demands on the reader and revealed a range of competency with the skill. National, state, or local guidelines such as the *Reading Development Checklist* published in the National Research Council Report on Preventing Reading Difficulties (http://www.readingsuccesslab.com/Reading_Development_Checklist.htm) provide a scale to determine a reader's level of performance based on a range of observed competencies and grade level expectations.

Drawing from several types of measures reinforces the principle that it's necessary to analyze multiple assessments from various sources and situations before making an evaluation. Even when made, evaluations are not written in stone. They reflect a conclusion at a given moment in time, based on evidence at hand. Each day, new experiences and learning change the landscape.

THE NEXT CHAPTER

Now that you've gathered and analyzed a myriad of rich data on a child's reading performance, you can reflect on how the pieces fit with previously gathered information and observations. What do they reveal about this child's strengths and needs at this point in time? What would be the most appropriate mediation/support that leads the reader to the next step in literacy development? Or, does this child need more practice with skills and strategies that are currently emerging?

Part IV of this text, "Differentiating Instruction Based on Data from Authentic Curriculum-Based Measures (Running Records)" begins with Chapter 7. The first aspect of teaching guided by RR assessment that's discussed is differentiating instruction for development in reading accuracy.

EXTENDING THE DISCUSSION

- View the videos of children reading and retelling at the website. Review the retelling checklist forms for each completed by the teacher. Discuss these with colleagues or classmates.
- Bring some of your own tapes and completed retelling checklists to a meeting or class. Collaboratively analyze your checklists after listening to the taped retelling with others.
- Describe your schedule for taking complete RRs or the schedule for doing this in classrooms where you've observed. How do you or did the teacher establish independent work protocols for other children (e.g. for centers or group work) that lessened interruptions while taking the RR?

Part IV

Differentiating Instruction Based on Data from Authentic Curriculum-Based Measures (Running Records)

7

DIFFERENTIATING INSTRUCTION
IN WORD READING

AN INTEGRATED STRATEGIES APPROACH
FOR DECODING

Teachers can usually sense by body language and voice when a reader is apprehensive about a big, scary word up ahead. The child slows down a tad; she may even repeat in order to get another running start at the nemesis. Teachers prepare children for such situations by emphasizing that the next word in any text they're reading can't be any word in the world.

Decoding is overwhelming for children who don't approach words with that understanding. The possibilities for any next word are actually narrow. It has to make sense and sound right in its place in a sentence. When the word sounds right, it follows the way we speak in our language.

Tell children that if they're thinking while reading, their brain is expecting the next word to be one of a few possible ones. When potential words are bouncing around in their brain, children's eyes will recognize which one the author used when they see the letters. Remind readers to *confirm* what they expected, checking that the letters in the target word are appropriate—all the way through from beginning to end—graphophonemically matching. It's equally important that readers simultaneously integrate other cues or clues; they need to consider the context. Does the word they are saying make sense (semantics)? Does it make the sentence sound right—the way we use words or string them together when we talk (syntax/grammar or language structure)?

If readers can't confirm what they expected, they need to reflect on the meaning and look more closely at the letters to decode words by *chunks* and sounds. It's easier to figure out a word by decoding bigger parts—chunks (i.e. syllables, phonograms). It might be a word the reader has never heard or a new use for a word he already knows. Refer back to step #2 in the CLUNK strategy (Figure 3.1).

In the *interactive strategies approach*, Scanlon, Anderson, and Sweeney (2010) emphasize the continuous interaction of cue systems by readers as they apply strategies to decode unknown words and construct meaning. Cecil (2007b) outlines a *whole-part-whole* instructional sequence for teaching phonics; it's also a sequence for decoding unknown words when reading. The order keeps the focus on comprehension.

When the child meets an unknown word, he reads the whole sentence, saying "Mmm" for the word before continuing to the end of the sentence (Figure 3.1). This allows him to grasp some context for the target word. If the word isn't recognized, the reader digs deeper into his repertoire of phonics and word structure knowledge to work out the word. When he thinks he knows the word, the child rereads the sentence to recapture the flow of meaning and check whether the word fits semantically and syntactically (grammatically). Instruction in phonetic and structural elements provides the tools needed for the medial part of the whole-part-whole sequence.

Key Concepts

Graphophonemic: referring to letters (graphemes) and sounds (phonemes) in a word.

Context: the situation, specific words, or behaviors that surround an oral or written message or statement and influence its meaning.

Phonogram: the rhyming part of a word, often referred to as word families or rimes (e.g. *at, et, in, and, ake, ack*).

Cue systems: the separate sources of clues or cues that help readers identify words. These include semantics, syntactic, and letter/sound cues.

Phonics: the relationship between letters and sounds in a language.

Word structure knowledge: understanding that words are constructed of parts such as onsets and rimes, root words, or root words with affixes (prefixes and/or suffixes).

ANALYZING PARTS OF WORDS

When children have acquired a minimal sight vocabulary from wide reading and writing (shared reading, independent reading, shared writing, independent writing), it's time to *show* them how readers use the words they know to figure out the ones they don't. This increases children's confidence with the task of solving word recognition and word construction problems when reading and writing.

This word comparison process that enhances readers' decoding fluency and independence is called *analytic phonics*. It differs from *synthetic phonics* methodology that teaches L-S relationships in isolation (Cunningham, 2005). In the analytic phonics approach children learn to notice word chunks (i.e. rimes, root words, affixes) and think about how these are similar to parts of known words; they use that awareness to figure out the new word with similar parts.

Reviewing concepts related to onsets and rimes as well as structural elements of words (e.g. prefix, suffix, root words, and syllables) helps struggling readers recognize word parts automatically. Interchanging onsets with a rime or matching a prefix (e.g. *re*, *un*) and/or suffix (e.g. *ful*, *ly*) with a root word when using flip books or flip wheels helps children build fluency in decoding longer words (Cecil, 2007b; Crawley, 2009). See Figure 7.1. When children instantly recognize rimes, they can use them as a foundation to read and spell multiple words that use the pattern. Children also learn how to manipulate structural elements of words—removing initial or ending parts and adding new ones. Such manipulation is characteristic in Reading Recovery sessions; it's called "making and breaking" (Clay, 1993b, p. 44). Teachers *make and break* words with children using magnetic letters, word pockets, or interactive whiteboards. See Figure 7.2. However, even after such practice, the length of a word might intimidate emergent readers.

Show children how to cover a word part in a word they are not recognizing with a thumb (or finger); this often allows a focus on the

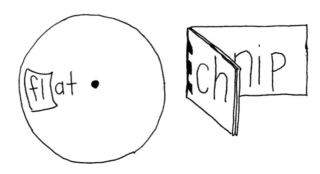

Flip books, flip wheel for onsets and rimes

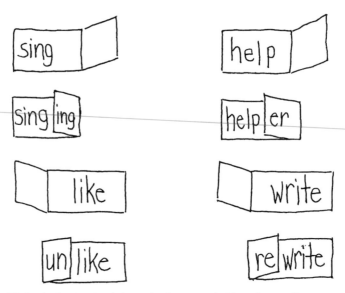

Flip books for structural elements of root word with prefix or suffix

Figure 7.1 Manipulatives for Recognizing Word Parts

root word. Eventually children don't need the physical cover on the word part. In the sentence—*The boy walked to the playground while other children were running to the swings*—there's a word with an added ending (walked), a compound word (playground), and a word that doubled the final consonant before adding the ending (running). See Figure 7.3. Decoding a familiar part can trigger recognition of the root word with additions. The child's level of sight vocabulary will be a critical factor for success with decoding new words.

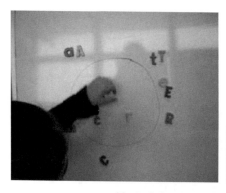

Manipulating magnetic letters

Making and breaking words on an interactive or regular whiteboard

Figure 7.2 Working with Words

Before children can manipulate a lot of words they need to have built a repertoire of sight, expressive, meaning, and automatic writing vocabulary; they use this knowledge when manipulating onsets and rimes, recognizing root words with and without additions, and as a basis for analytical phonics. Effective teachers make lists and display words children have learned by word solving; these provide readers with visible evidence of their achievement.

COLLECTING WORDS LEARNED

Teachers at all grade levels use word walls as a reference for children when reading or writing (Crawley, 2009). See Figure 7.4. Children refer to the word wall independently when decoding (recognizing words) or encoding (writing); sometimes the teacher reviews lists of words with

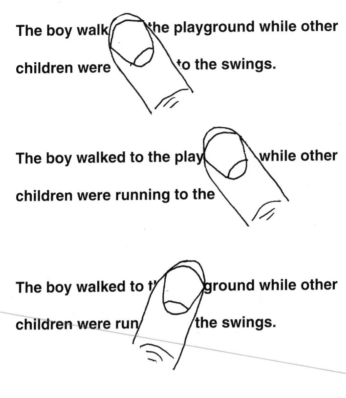

The boy walk⬭the playground while other children were ⬭to the swings.

The boy walked to the play⬭while other children were running to the ⬭

The boy walked to t⬭ground while other children were run⬭the swings.

The boy walked to the playground while other children were run ⬭the swings.

Figure 7.3 Using a Thumb Cover to Focus on Root Words or Components of a Compound Word

small groups or the class. These are very simple in primary grades and more sophisticated in middle and upper elementary.

The word wall should be placed where all students can easily view it. Teachers use a bulletin board, chart paper, or pocket charts to display words. Many primary classrooms have an alphabetically organized

Key Concepts

Shared writing: the teacher writes a message in front of children, verbalizing the process of composing, including thought generation, spelling words, and rereading the constructed message. Children are encouraged to interject help with suggestions for ideas and word construction. The class reads the completed message.

Analytic phonics: after building a bank of known words, children analyze them to determine phonics generalizations.

Reading Recovery: structured intervention protocol for struggling readers delivered by highly trained teachers in a one-to-one instructional setting.

Making and breaking: given a word with an onset and rime, students remove the onset (break) and substitute another one (make) to spell a new word. Given a root word, students add and change affixes (prefix or suffix) to make and break words.

Synthetic phonics: children learn letter/sound associations in the language and then apply this knowledge to learn words.

Onset: beginning letter (or letters) in a word that precede(s) the rime (phonogram or word family part). In the word *black*, *bl* is the onset and *ack* is the rime, word family, or phonogram.

Sight vocabulary/sight words: words the reader recognizes on sight when reading. These can be high frequency ones or any other words in the language.

Expressive vocabulary: words the child uses appropriately in oral communication (talking).

Meaning vocabulary: words for which the child understands a meaning—a listening vocabulary. These may or may not be words the child uses in speech.

Automatic writing vocabulary: words a child can write automatically from memory—without having to sound out each part.

Alphabetically organized word wall

Topic specific word wall

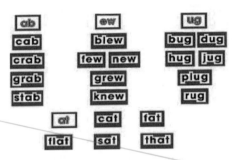

Word families (rimes, phonograms) word walls

Synonym word wall

Individual word wall folder

Figure 7.4 Word Walls

word wall; the first words typically added in an early childhood classroom are children's names. These are placed under the first letter of the child's name (Morrow, 2007). As new words—particularly high frequency (HF) words—are introduced in shared reading, Language Experience activities, or collaborative writing, the teacher and/or students select ones to be added to the word wall. The new addition is written on a card; then it's read, sounded, spelled, and read again before it's posted on the wall. However, word walls can also be organized topically or display onset and rime lists; they can also act as a mini thesaurus, offering interesting synonyms for words over-worked in writing. Effective teachers display words strategically and change word lists to support current instructional goals. Individualized word wall folders alphabetically organize word lists for children to use as a reference when reading or writing; these include HF words as well as personally requested words.

Selected HF words are ones typically found on the Dolch or Fry lists of HF words (Dolch, 1936; Fry, 1999). Go to http://www.mrsperkins.com/dolch.htm for the Dolch HF word list and http://www.candohelperpage.com/sightvocab_1.html or http://www.uniqueteachingresources.com/Fry-1000-Instant-Words.html for the Fry HF word list. For additional lists of words, go to http://www.janbrett.com/games/high_frequency_word_list_main.htm; you can download five printable lists for the first 100 HF words (with 20 words per list).

Other words added to word walls are ones related to specific areas of interest or study—ones the teacher or children feel are important to have posted. The HF words vary in spelling complexity; some are more abstract in meaning, making them harder to remember. Frequent reading and writing of HF words in continuous text increases the likelihood that they'll become sight words for children.

One HF word cannot be decoded phonetically (i.e. *of*); other HF words have limited letter/sound matching (e.g. *was*). Some HF words can be partially sounded through (e.g. *said*); other words can be decoded by L-S matching combined with useful phonics generalizations (e.g. *pick, way, far, cat, make*). See Figure 7.5. Effective teachers build children's phonetic and word structure knowledge across many mini lessons; topics for these reflect needs identified in assessments and careful observations. However, neither the phonetic knowledge nor the strategy taught in a mini lesson is an end in itself; each is a means to the goal. Children are expected to *use* the skill or strategy with automaticity as they fluently read and comprehend text—returning to the *whole* after working with *parts* (whole-part-whole).

1. When *r* comes after a vowel, the vowel sound is neither long nor short; it's a vowel *controlled* by r (e.g. *car, star, for, fir*).
2. Words that have a double *e* have a long sound for that vowel pair (e.g. *weed, beet*).
3. The letter patterns *ay, ey,* and *eigh* are usually sounded as a long *a* (e.g. *day, play, they, prey, eight, neighbor*).
4. When *y* is the last letter of a word, it usually has a vowel sound. It's sounded as a long *i* in shorter words (i.e. *my, fry*) and as a long *e* in longer words (e.g. *baby, puppy*).
5. When *c* and *h* are next to each other they make one sound. It's a new sound (e.g. *chair*) or the sound of *k* (e.g. *character*). When *s* and *h* are next to each other they make one sound. It's a new sound (e.g. *show, share*).
6. When *th* and *wh* are together they make a single sound (e.g. *that, this, when, whale*).
7. When *kn, gn, mn,* and *ph* come together they make one sound; it's the sound of one of them (e.g. *knee, gnat, hymn*) or the sound of a different letter (e.g. *phone*).
8. When *c* is followed by *e, i,* or *y,* it usually has the *s* sound (e.g. *circus, cycle*). When *c* is followed by *o* or *a,* it usually has the *k* sound (e.g. *coat, color*).
9. When *g* is followed by *e, i,* or *y,* it usually has the *j* sound (e.g. *gym, gem*).
10. Sometimes *s* can have the *z* sound (e.g. *boys, girls*) or the *sh* sound (e.g. *sure, sugar*).
11. When *igh* is in a word, it's sounded as long *i* (e.g. *bright, might*).
12. When *ck* comes at the end of a word it's sounded as *k* (e.g. *check, track*).
13. In most two syllable words the first syllable is *accented* or stressed in speech (i.e. *mon*-key, *li*-on).
14. If *a, in, re, de,* or *be* is the first syllable in a word, it's usually *unaccented* (e.g. *begin, decide*).
15. In most two-syllable words that end in a consonant followed by *y,* the first syllable is accented (e.g. *baby, puppy*).
16. If the last syllable ends with *le,* the consonant preceding the *le* begins the last syllable (e.g. *table*).
17. When the first vowel in a word is followed by *ch, th,* or *sh,* these consonant pairs are not split when the word is divided into syllables (e.g. *teacher*).
18. When there is only one vowel in a word that ends with a consonant, that vowel is usually sounded with a short sound (e.g. *bed, cat*).
19. When a vowel is the last letter in a syllable it is usually sounded with a long sound (i.e. ba-*by,* li-*on*); this is an *open* syllable.
20. When a consonant is the last letter of a syllable; the vowel before it usually has the short sound (i.e. *pup*-py). This is a *closed* syllable.

Figure 7.5 Twenty Useful Phonics Generalizations
Source Adapted from Cecil, 2007b, p. 86

Key Concepts

Word wall: a display of words learned. These can be alphabetically arranged or organized as a collection of words (i.e. related to a topic, associated with a rime, or synonyms for a target word).

High frequency (HF) word: a word that appears very often in a text.

Language Experience: a protocol for shared writing. The class discusses a shared event or a few children describe a personal one. The teacher scribes the words dictated by children and the class reads the text created.

Collaborative writing: the teacher and children collaboratively construct a text. They share ideas and plan together; the teacher scribes most of this text, but also invites children to write out words or phrases.

Continuous text: prose (e.g. sentences, paragraphs, verse) constructed for the purpose of communicating ideas. It can be in the form of story, informational writing, essay, or poetry.

Mini lesson: instructional sequence containing all of the components (e.g. introduction, instruction, guided practice, independent practice, closure, and assessment) of an effective lesson. However, the narrowly defined objective allows the interaction to be targeted and brief.

Automaticity: the ability to do something without having to occupy the mind with details related to the task. The task is performed as an automatic response pattern.

Phonics generalization: a statement about particular letter/sound relationships in the language that applies to many words. It's not categorized as a rule since many words in English maintain letter/sound correspondence and patterns from their derivational source rather than adhering to a generalization for the English language.

MANY MINI LESSONS FOR WORD STUDY

Review the decoding mini lesson at the companion website as well; it focuses on word analogy as a decoding strategy. Go to http://www2. scholastic.com/browse/article.jsp?id=4494; view a lesson on short vowels (*Another Bag Full of Vowel Sounds*) with a child who disregards medial sounds when decoding words. A lesson plan at http://www. halcyon.com/marcs/decode.html can be implemented with a small group.

It guides children through the process of using multiple cue systems. Adding a bit of technology to the practice can be highly motivating; review the lesson with interactive computer word sorts at http://www.readwritethink.org/classroom-resources/lesson-plans/word-sorts-beginning-struggling-795.html. Figure 7.6 lists websites that offer a myriad of resources for word study. You'll find resources readily available to support word study in classrooms across many levels. Plan your own mini lessons based on observations and assessment of readers in your class. What do they need to know? What are they doing, but confusing?

Some readers begin to integrate cues (clues) embedded in the text intuitively. They use the flow of meaning and their background knowledge for literary language and decode words that the teacher expected would be difficult. After the reading, draw children's attention to words they decoded *on-the-run* (automatically). Specifically, help readers reflect on strategies used; help them articulate those processes. You also want to draw visual attention to the full word to ensure readers know each after decoding it; children should be able to use newly decoded words for speaking and writing as well as recognize them in other contexts.

The Internet has numerous resources of lessons, center activities, and games that have the potential to build and reinforce word recognition fluency when used effectively. Be discriminating or intelligently eclectic; choose instructionally sound ideas that match your philosophy of teaching and learning.

Phonics: printable worksheets and activities (word families)
http://www.kidzone.ws/phonics/index.htm

Word sorts
http://www.stoughton.k12.wi.us/webpages/bbarberino/homeworkhappenings.cfm?subpage=1089254

Computer interactive sorts
http://www.eduplace.com/kids/sv/books/content/wordsort

Word recognition building activities and video of children engaged in word reading activities
http://www.readingresource.net/readingactivities-II.html

Games that build word recognition fluency
http://www.readingresource.net/reading-games.html

Figure 7.6 Resources for Building Decoding Skills

Sometimes, good readers don't absorb new words or use them in their own compositions. They may be good readers, but poor spellers because they don't notice words they've decoded effortlessly (Scott, 1993). In word study and discussion, focus on drawing readers' attention to the distinguishing features of a target word while constantly attaching meaning in the immediate and other contexts (Kibby, 1989). Make a note of these decoding situations. It becomes the content of a teaching point after the RR or a mini lesson for a small group. Effective word study involves an *integrated* examination of words; it's broader than instruction in phonics and/or structural analysis alone. It's a process that ensures that readers simultaneously build both vocabulary knowledge and word recognition skills necessary for fluent reading and full comprehension.

Key Concepts

Distinguishing features: distinctive word parts, shape and length (configuration), letter patterns, and meaning associations that support rapid recognition of the word.

Word study: an integrated approach to building vocabulary knowledge and decoding skills (e.g. those associated with phonetic and structural analysis). Word study reinforces an integrated use of the cue systems.

BACK TO THE WHOLE: DECODING AUTOMATICALLY AND INTEGRATIVELY WHILE READING

To understand what you want children to be able to do, consider what proficient readers do. That's the target behavior you want each child to reach. Proficient readers process meaning as they go. They expect the words that are coming next. Consider the following sentences with missing words.

There is no such _____ as monsters under the bed. But, whenever I heard strange n-----, I would feel a little a-----. I would call M--. ___would come to my ____. "T----'s nothing u---- your ___", she'd ___. "I'll look right n-- for ___."

(There is no such thing as monsters under the bed. But, whenever I heard strange noises, I would feel a little afraid. I would call Mom. She would come to my room. "There's nothing under your bed," she'd say. "I'll look right now for you.")

When you got to the spaces, you probably read right through. Sometimes an initial letter and word length was all you needed for confirmation; other times, not even that was necessary. The familiarity of the phrase was enough to trigger recognition. Proficient readers don't analyze every letter of every word on the page. It would take forever to finish if they did. They use contextual meaning, vocabulary knowledge, word structure, configuration (e.g. shape, length), and letter/sound associations interactively—integratively.

Only when our eyes catch a difference in letters used—where we expected a particular word—do we stop and say, "Whoa! What was that?" We go back, reread, and correct. You might have read *bedroom* for *room* in the third sentence—a longer word for the configuration presented by the actual word. That miscue would not have interrupted meaning. Proficient readers aim for accuracy. However, when made, seemingly slight changes in wording can create shades of differences in meaning. Still, it's important to remain selective when drawing attention to miscues that don't significantly affect meaning during the reading.

Proficient readers process meaning while decoding. Combined, semantic and syntactic cues create what we call *context clues*. As a speaker, young readers know how words are ordered in a sentence even though they don't know the terminology for English language conventions. That structure or grammar—including order, tense, and parts of speech—is syntax. Young children also recognize literary language.

Children internalize literary phrases in books read aloud. The word patterns become so familiar as to be instantly decodable when met in print. These children decode "Once upon a time ..." or "And, they lived happily ever after" with ease.

Context clues integrated with background knowledge and experience help the proficient reader narrow down the possibilities for an unknown word; it's within a range of words that would *make sense* and *sound right* (Clay, 2001). Then, the proficient reader visually scans letters used in the author's word—beginning to end—as well as its length and shape. After that instant perusal, the proficient reader confirms which one of expected words the author used. This process—from initiation to conclusion—needs to be repeatedly demonstrated for novice readers.

Key Concept

Context clues: the combination of word usage, form (e.g. tense, number), and order in a sentence (or segment of text) that relates to semantics (meaning) and syntax (grammar).

MODELING DECODING STRATEGIES AND MORE

Strategic teachers model a variety of strategies used for decoding new words when they're reading aloud to children. They do this nonchalantly, verbalizing thinking as they work through the process of figuring out a word. It's as though listeners are eavesdropping on the teacher's thinking. But, teachers also accomplish so many other objectives through their read-alouds. They introduce children to wonderful stories and books—ones that spark curiosity and expand background knowledge. That knowledge supports readers' ability to use context clues for decoding new words. Exposure to different kinds of text structures builds a mental framework that children can draw upon when reading themselves. Finally, teachers infuse lovely, powerful words into children's listening vocabularies when they hear quality literature. Those words will be easier to decode when first met in print.

Many of the teacher's word-decoding demonstrations are staged— preplanned. But, there are times when she really does trip over words. These provide unexpected opportunities to talk about how she noticed and self-corrected a mistake. After much modeling and discussion, students try to independently apply the strategies demonstrated.

GUIDING AND SCAFFOLDING STUDENTS' USE OF STRATEGIES

Model—one by one—each strategy on the posters found at http://www. smbsd.org/page.cfm?p=2419 (click on phonics poster) or http://www. mrsbunyi.com/decoding_strategies.html. (The posters and source can be found at the companion website.) You can exaggerate the strategy to make it obvious; ask children to describe what they saw you do.

Have children discuss what they saw as you modeled the strategy; explain your behavior. Then, introduce the poster for that particular strategy.

Practice the strategy together; have children practice it with a partner. Then, ask them to use it when reading independently. These steps are repeated for each strategy.

Allow children to use the reading strategies bookmark as a guide and support after all the strategies are introduced. (See Figure 7.7.) At the end of independent reading time, have children share the strategies they used while reading. It's always interesting to hear about individual strategy selections and the rationale for each. The discussion

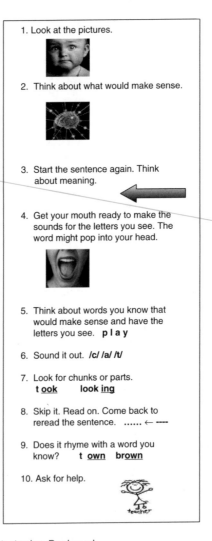

1. Look at the pictures.

2. Think about what would make sense.

3. Start the sentence again. Think about meaning.

4. Get your mouth ready to make the sounds for the letters you see. The word might pop into your head.

5. Think about words you know that would make sense and have the letters you see. **p l a y**

6. Sound it out. **/c/ /a/ /t/**

7. Look for chunks or parts. **t ook   look ing**

8. Skip it. Read on. Come back to reread the sentence. **...... ← ----**

9. Does it rhyme with a word you know? **t own   brown**

10. Ask for help.

Figure 7.7 Reading Strategies Bookmark

develops metacognition and further demystifies the word solving process.

The strategies soon become part of the class's shared knowledge—their reading terminology. You can reference them on the posters around the room or on the bookmark a child is using. When working with a reader who stops at a word, remain silent. Wait to see what she'll do. If nothing happens after a reasonable pause, ask, "What can you do?" Suggest that she tries her plan. If that doesn't work, ask, "What can you try now?" The goal is to be a *guide-on-the-side* as the reader decides which tools to use and gets the job done. Giving too much assistance creates learned helplessness. You want the child to take control—to be a word solver when she meets a tricky word that was unexpected.

Every once in a while, an author surprises his/her reader. A word like *picayune* provided a perfect example. A teacher shared the following story as an example for readers in her class.

> The word *picayune* was one I had only heard; I'd never seen it. One day while reading a novel, I was expecting the next word in the sentence to be trivial, unimportant, or insignificant due to the contextual clues I'd gathered. However, I was stopped dead in my tracks by the letters I saw. None of the words I expected could be confirmed. I had to use visual (graphophonemic—L-S) cues (clues). I'd never seen this word in print. I decoded it—/pic/—/a/— /yoon/.
>
> "Oh, my gosh!" I said to myself. "It's *picayune*!" I looked it up because I was so curious. Its origin is French (*picaillon*) for half pence. A Spanish coin used in Louisiana and other southern states (half dime) was called a picayune. It does mean trivial or of little value—like the coins. When I made my mouth say and blend the sounds represented by the letters, I got close enough to recognize the word that was in my speaking vocabulary—a word I knew. It fitted meaningfully—semantically. It sounded right in the sentence. It fit syntactically—grammatically—and the letters were appropriate; it *was* picayune.
>
> I was integrating the cue systems when I decoded *picayune*. I started with meaning (semantics) and structure (grammar or syntax) to apply context clues. I was expecting possible words that would make sense and sound right. I tried to confirm one of my expectations with visual clues. When I couldn't do that, I closely analyzed the anomaly—this unexpected configuration or shape of letters (visual clues)—to decode a word I'd heard but never met in print.

That behavior is what I want you to do as readers. You need to self-initiate or start that kind of thinking for yourself when you meet a new word. Just saying it after figuring out the sounds is not enough. You often need to adjust what you said based on sounds because the word is following sound patterns from its original source. Thinking about the meaning in the text helps trigger recognition of the word as you know it or have heard it spoken. If it's a word that you've never heard, you can use context to figure out what it means in the situation and check the pronunciation later—in a dictionary or by asking someone for help.

Key Concept

Metacognition: thinking about one's thinking, the cognitive activity involved in a task, or the plan for accomplishing an objective.

PROMOTING SELF-INITIATED USE OF STRATEGIES

As proficient readers, integration of cues systems happens seamlessly for teachers. They hardly direct it; they just do it. This level of operation is a result of extensive reading. It's like riding a bike or driving a car. One has to perform the behavior over and over under multiple conditions to develop proficiency and independence. But, the reader must know most of the words around the unknown word to use context clues for decoding it fluently.

Readers can't integrate cue systems when the text is at their frustrational level. Children placed in frustrational level text only use visual clues. They're unable to narrow down possibilities; they haven't gathered enough meaning to do that since many words are unknown. Working continuously in frustrational level text leaves readers with only one cue system for decoding.

Children need opportunities for guided and independent practice before they're expected to self-initiate decoding strategies. Use instructional level text for guided reading and easy text for independent reading. Provide *lots* of time for practice; meeting HF words repeatedly in meaningful text is the best way for children to learn them. Children also build sight vocabulary for reading and writing through word games. You'll find a list of websites with sight word building activities at the companion website. Refer to the list in Figure 7.6 as well. See Figure 7.8 for rhyming activities. Effective teachers also involve children in writing, including journaling, responding to literature, or taking notes in content areas.

Down by the Bay

(Traditional song.)

Down by the bay where the watermelons grow,

Back to my home I dare not go.

For if I do my mother will say,

"Did you ever see a bear combing his hair down by the bay?

Did you ever see a bee with a sunburned knee down by the bay?"

Adapting text with rhyming add-ons: Students and teacher make up lines, extending mother's questions. These can be recorded for singing and reading.

"Did you ever see a cat fixing a flat down by the bay?

Did you ever see a cow taking a bow down by the bay?"

Rhyme Hunts

The teacher or child says,
"A hunting I will go.
A hunting I will go.
Hi ho the derry-o.
A hunting I will go.
I'm hunting for a word.
That rhymes with _____."

A student answers,
"It could be _____."

Another student adds,
"It could be _____."

Figure 7.8 Playing with Rimes
Source Raffi, 1987; adapted from Crawley, 2009, p. 33

Writing involves encoding (constructing words) at the L-S, onset-rime, or root-affix level; this involves complex thinking and multiple associations. Writing makes words increasingly automatic—children can write them from memory. When children can write a word, they can read it (Bissex, 1980). Writing increases children's sight vocabulary; it also builds their automatic writing vocabulary (Shea, 2011). Research concludes a reciprocal nature in learning to read and write—growth in one language process fuels growth in the other (Bissex, 1980; Cecil, 2007b; Clay, 1980; Whitmore, Martens, Goodman, & Owocki, 2005). Children with strong sight and writing vocabularies are more likely to recognize miscues and apply fix-up strategies in reading and writing.

CELEBRATING SELF-MONITORING
AND SELF-CORRECTING

Continuously demonstrate how you monitor your reading by stopping when meaning is lost. Problem-solve out loud, looking for the source of confusion. Say, "Sometimes I have to correct a miscue." Talking through your thinking helps children appreciate the problem-solving required for fluent reading.

In debriefing conversations that follow a RR, always compliment the reader's self-correcting. You might comment, "You noticed that something didn't make sense right here and went back to reread and correct it. That's what good readers do." Readers are likely to repeat behaviors that are celebrated. Teachers should also comment on self-monitoring and self-correcting when working with groups of children.

When children are reading together in guided reading groups or as a class, draw attention to *in-action* (while reading) exemplars of self-monitoring and self-correcting. Talk about how these miscue corrections made the reading smoother and the information easier to understand. Such conversation positively recognizes readers for their hard work and reinforces the expectation for self-initiation and use of decoding strategies whenever the need arises.

The next chapter talks about differentiating for fluency. Abundant independent reading with comfortable (e.g. familiar) books will build fluency as well as sight vocabulary and decoding skills. The simple practice has powerful, multi-faceted results.

EXTENDING THE DISCUSSION

- Review the decoding posters and websites for sight word building, and decoding bookmark at the companion website. Discuss how these can be used at your grade level.

- Have a conversation with colleagues about children's ability or reluctance to self-initiate strategies. How can scaffolds be built for those reluctant to self-initiate word solving and faded once they get started? Monitor the child's progress in self-initiating strategies taught. What works? What doesn't work?
- Share ideas for inexpensive sight word games for parents and children to play at home. Provide parents with materials or a list of websites.

8

DIFFERENTIATING INSTRUCTION
IN FLUENCY

COMPONENTS OF FLUENCY

The fluency assessment part of a complete RR directs attention to the multiple, essential components of the trait, assuring that each area will be evaluated. Refer back to the fluency checklist (i.e. #8 in Figure 3.2) used with the RR; determine where the child needs assistance. Is the weakness in word recognition? Does the reader need to learn strategies that will facilitate *word reading accuracy* and *automaticity*? Or, is the problem with other aspects of fluency (e.g. phrasing, expression, pitch)? Differentiating instruction for automatic word reading accuracy was discussed in Chapter 7—accuracy as related to the percent of correctness in decoding (word reading) and automaticity as characterized by rapid and effortless recognition of words. This chapter will mainly focus on the other aspects of fluency.

Does the child read in a *monotone voice* without injecting expression—without appropriate *prosody*? Does the expectation of the task make him uncomfortable? Are words read in meaningful phrases or meaning units (Young & Rasinski, 2009)? Target instruction where it's needed; group children for mini lessons on specific aspects of fluency. See Figure 8.1. Too often, the only aspect of fluency that's emphasized, practiced, and assessed is speed (e.g. with WCPM). When that happens, children get the wrong message. They begin to assume that speed is the primary goal—that faster reading is better reading regardless of other factors, including comprehension.

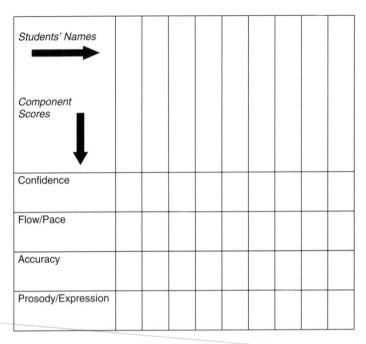

Figure 8.1 Grouping for Fluency Instruction

Key Concepts

Monotone voice: series of words spoken in a similar tone of voice (e.g. without expression, intonation).

Prosody: a composite of multiple features (e.g. rhythm, phrasing, stress, emotion, and intonation) in speech.

Intonation: variance in pitch when speaking. It involves a rising or falling pitch (e.g. expressing surprise, ending a thought).

Stress: emphasis given to certain syllables, words, phrases, or sentences when speaking.

Phrasing: grouping words in meaningful units (e.g. in the dark, dark woods, once upon a time) when speaking or reading them.

COUNTERING THE NASCAR READER EFFECT

Instead of creating *NASCAR readers*—ones who practice reading with a narrow focus on speed—invite children to engage in authentic reasons for rereading texts. Rereading leads to smooth reading and deeper comprehension (Shea, 2006, 2011). Reckless speed actually inhibits efficient reading. The unintended consequence of focusing on WCPM when practicing for fluency has encouraged students to read with speed regardless of their degree of comprehension (Rasinski, 2006). "Many students come to identify fast reading as proficient reading. This, we feel, is a disturbing and unwarranted approach to fluency instruction" (Young & Rasinski, 2009, p. 5).

Key Concept

NASCAR readers: readers who race through text, saying the words as quickly as possible.

IMPORTANCE OF ORAL FLUENCY

Much reading is done orally with young children. It allows the teacher to monitor and guide their text processing. Although they soon learn to internalize reading, many children continue to *mumble read* for a while.

Usually, these mumble readers think they're reading to themselves—in their head. When asked, "Are you reading silently?" a child will enthusiastically nod his head to indicate, "Yes, of course." It amazes teachers how the little hum in a group of *not so silent* silent readers fails to distract anyone. But, one might wonder why there's an emphasis on increasing oral reading fluency if reading is mostly done silently beyond primary grades. Mumble reading or subvocalizing may continue even when children have learned to read silently; it usually occurs when they meet text that's particularly challenging (i.e. dense with information) (Bruinsma, 1980). Teachers encourage students "to subvocalize or even vocalize in order to have direct auditory aid to the processing of prose" (Bruinsma, 1980, p. 294); they expect that the practice will naturally lessen in time—as reading proficiency increases (Bruinsma, 1980).

Researchers report a strong positive correlation between oral reading fluency and silent reading comprehension (Daane, Campbell, Grigg,

Goodman, & Oranje, 2005; Pinnell et al., 1995). These findings led to the conclusion that oral fluency translates to being fluent in silent reading (Reutzel, Jones, Fawson, & Smith, 2008).

Students who read aloud with accuracy, automaticity, confidence, prosody, and expression tend to understand what they read both orally *and* silently; the reverse has also been reported (Young & Rasinski, 2009). Disfluent oral readers are more likely to have weaker comprehension when reading silently. Fluent reading—in oral and silent modes—has far reaching effects for learning and achievement.

Studies have examined a variety of approaches that demonstrate positive results for developing reading fluency. Additionally, the same methods that are effective in increasing fluency with non-ELLs (English Language Learners) are recommended for ELLs (August & Shanahan, 2006; Vaughn, Mathes, Linan-Thompson, Cirino, Carlson, & Pollard-Durodola, 2006). Purposeful rereading is central to many of these fluency building activities that all begin with teacher modeling.

Key Concepts

Mumble read: read orally, but in a whisper or very low voice.

Subvocalize: movement of the lips when reading in order to imagine the sounds of words and/or feel the mouth's formation of them. Sometimes, words mouthed are slightly audible. Subvocalization can also be inner speech when reading.

REREADING FOR A PURPOSE

Rereading builds fluency; it also deepens comprehension. Routman (2003) noted, "rereading is the strategy most useful to readers of all ages. When given opportunities to reread material, readers' comprehension always goes up" (p. 122). But, it should be done with a genuine purpose (Altwerger, Jordan, & Shelton, 2007). When reading aloud, model rereading to clarify a part that was confusing or contained many details that were difficult to recall. Rereading allows the reader to focus on content since the words were decoded in the first read. Model how you revisit a text to find evidence that supports an interpretation. Reread that part aloud to emphasize your point. Conclusions drawn from any reading are more persuasive when they're well supported with details from the source. These demonstrations exemplify that deep comprehension often requires revisiting areas of the text (Altwerger et al., 2007; Fountas & Pinnell, 2006).

When reading a text together as a class, have children assume the role of rereading for the same purposes you modeled when reading aloud. Lots of guided experiences stimulate internalization of these practices. The benefits reach beyond fluency; comprehension is improved as well as children's ability to articulate a rationale for their ideas.

Rereading gives the brain additional time and information for processing; readers assimilate (take in) and accommodate (fit into existing schemata—background knowledge) the information presented in a text. Readers may also review visuals provided by the author, re-examine new words or uses for known ones, and notice the writing craft in this segment when they've been taught to use rereading for such purposes. Students can reread independently and silently or with recorded material (i.e. CDs or DVDs). They follow along with a copy of the text while listening to the reader on the tape. Rereading in any format:

- deepens comprehension;
- increases vocabulary knowledge;
- draws attention to text visuals that augment understanding;
- offers time to savor the impact of sentence variety and word choice;
- allows students to learn from repetition.

Sometimes texts are reread more than once. Repeated readings of continuous text build fluency, word reading accuracy and automaticity, sight vocabulary, and reading confidence (Neumann, Ross, & Slaboch, 2008; Samuels, 1979).

Repeated reading of text also helps students become more familiar with the author's choice of words and patterns of expression. Readers increase their understanding of the topic, adding to their schema (background knowledge) related to it. They better understand new words or known words used in a new way. Reading words in continuous text rather than on lists or in isolation strengthens sight vocabulary; it's easier to remember words and more motivating to read them when the task involves interesting text.

SIGHT VOCABULARY, HIGH FREQUENCY WORDS

As previously discussed in Chapter 7, words recognized automatically—without excessive attention to separate letters—and accurately on sight are referred to as one's sight vocabulary. There are several lists of HF words (McKenna & Stahl, 2003). The Dolch and Fry lists were suggested in Chapter 7. As well as frequently reading these words in meaningful text, daily personal writing ensures that words are well learned (Shea, 2011). Daily personal writing contributes to automatic word recognition and accuracy—an essential first step for fluency.

Kindergarteners are expected to learn 24 HF words, first graders 100 words, second graders 200 words, and third graders 300 words (Tompkins, 2010). Pinnell and Fountas (1998, p. 89) list the 24 HF words that kindergarten children should learn through experiences with print. These are:

a	at	he	it	no	the
am	can	I	like	see	to
an	do	in	me	she	up
and	go	is	my	so	we

Eldredge (2005) found that the 300 highest-frequency words accounted for 72% of words used in first grade basal readers and trade books for that level. It's important that children learn to read and write these words. But that's not easy, since many of them do not follow expected sound-symbol relationships as noted in Chapter 7.

Repetition is necessary to learn HF words. But, effective teachers discourage practice that involves the isolated repetition of words. The importance of meeting words repeatedly in meaningful text and using them often in personal writing cannot be overemphasized; it helps children own them and facilitates reading them in meaningful units—in phrases. Appropriate phrasing is central to fluency—fluency characterized by the accurate reading of words in meaningful strings (Shea, 2006). See Figure 8.2.

Finally, rereading dense or confusing segments of a text has a positive impact on reading further passages even when later segments are not reread (Therrien & Kubina, 2007); the process creates understanding for what comes later. Appreciating the multiple benefits of meaningful repeated reading, teachers design varied activities that incorporate this into guided and independent practice.

REREADING COLLABORATIVELY

Sometimes children work with a more fluent peer to engage in *paired repeated reading* (Nichols, Rupley, & Rasinski, 2009). During such reading, children work with a partner to reread a text; they take turns reading (e.g. paragraph by paragraph or page by page). Paired repeated

Read this sentence word by word.

```
The ... small ... boy ... quickly ... ran ... to ... the ... new ... slide.
```

It's difficult to grasp meaning. You're anxiously waiting for each next word, hoping that it'll help you make sense of what you have so far. It's like a game of charades—working with the smallest units—word by word—trying to grasp the whole.

Try reading the sentence with an attempt to chunk words.

```
The small ... boy ... quickly ... ran to ... the new ... slide.
```

Understanding is still an effort. You're trying to merge semi-chunked bits together as you read along. That's extra and needless cognitive work before you can think about overall meaning.

Now read it chunked this way ...

```
The small boy ... quickly ran ... to the new slide.
```

and, then, this way ...

```
The small boy/quickly ran to the new slide.
```

Try it with a little addition. There's more to get in one breath, but it sounds natural when it's done that way.

```
The small boy/quickly ran to the new slide in the school playground.
```

When the words are recognized effortlessly and read accurately in meaningful units like this, understanding is seamless.

Figure 8.2 Chunking Words into Meaningful Phrases
Source Adapted from Shea, 2006, p. 75

reading increases both readers' fluency and confidence (with reading and/or performing). It also frees up cognitive energy for comprehension practice: each partner can apply learned strategies while listening (Topping, 2006). Children learn to work together and learn from each other. When one child is stuck on a word, the other reader acts as a teacher, suggesting a strategy and supporting his partner's independent use of it rather than telling him the word. If this doesn't work, the child as "teacher" gives his partner the word, but also demonstrates the suggested strategy for figuring it out.

Echo reading is another technique use to support disfluent readers; it starts at the sentence level (Cecil, 2007b). The more fluent reader models how the sentence should sound with regard to phrasing, intonation, expression, and flow. The partner repeats the sentence, attempting to replicate the model. Partners can also reread the text chorally or chorally with a recording. The recording provides a scaffold for new text as well as a model of how reading should sound.

For individual practice or practice at home, quality recorded texts provide exemplars of fluency. Children listen to the recording while following along with the text. In a reread, they whisper read along with the tape, attempting to mimic the reader's performance. This practice is referred to as *assisted reading*. Children can repeat the process until they independently read the text with accuracy, fluency, and understanding (Gilbert, Williams, & McLaughlin, 1996).

Competence grows as children realize the power of rereading with continuous text. Full fluency naturally becomes part of their repertoire of strategies for efficient reading (D'Angelo, 1979; Millis & King, 2001).

Research concludes that rereading leads to fluency on the texts reread as well as new texts—ones not previously encountered (Rasinski & Hoffman, 2003). Measuring fluency components on the checklist previously introduced (i.e. in Chapter 5) and calculating WCPM on taped readings as described provides valid, reliable documentation of fluency growth. Making the practice enjoyable ensures mindful engagement as opposed to rote practice.

Adding the dimension of performing for audiences gives rereading added purpose and excitement. Dramatic experiences yield personal benefits as well; they build confidence with public speaking and self-esteem (Clementi, 2010).

READERS' THEATER: FROM SIMPLE TO SOPHISTICATED

After the teacher has introduced a book for shared reading, done the first read as a model, and stimulated a meaningful discussion of its content, children are invited to reread the text with her. That practice yields all the benefits of rereading listed previously, but it can also become a script for dramatic performing (Clementi, 2010). It transforms to a simplified *readers' theater* (RT) as the teacher assigns pages for choral reading and dialog to individual readers. However, beyond simple dramatic rereading during shared reading, the activity can become a bit more of a production—a mini theatrical performance.

More involved RT involves a dramatic enactment of a story or information reporting from a script. See Figure 8.3 for a list of readers' theater scripts. Scripts can be purchased or constructed from the content of texts read (trade books or textbooks)—especially ones with lots of dialog or content that can easily be dramatized (Clementi, 2010). Since roles in any script vary in length and difficulty, it's possible to have mixed ability readers appropriately matched with text in the same script. The performance can be from a single script or

Websites with Free Scripts

http://www.readinglady.com/index.php?name=Downloads&req=viewdownload&cid=7
Pages and pages of readers' theater scripts to download

http://www.aaronshepard.com/
Another great site with tips on using RT.

http://www.teachingheart.net/readerstheater.htm
Lots of different resources; appropriate for all ages.

http://loiswalker.com/catalog/guidesamples.html

http://richmond.k12.va.us/readamillion/readerstheater.htm

http://www.timrasinski.com

http://www.cdli.ca/CITE/langrt.htm

http://www.educationworld.com/a_curr/reading/index.shtml#theater
A few holiday and fractured fairy tales.

http://pbskids.org/zoom/activities/playhouse/
Readers' Theater scripts from PBS.

http://www.myteacherpages.com/webpages/JGriffin/readers.cfm
Several short readers' theater scripts.

www.fictionteachers.com/classroomtheater/theater.html

Figure 8.3 Readers' Theater Scripts
Source http://www.mandygregory.com/readers_theater.htm, retrieved March 27, 2010; Young and Rasinski, 2009, pp. 4–13

children can work in small groups on multiple shorter performances. Flexible grouping ensures that children experience several models of fluency and acting styles (Casey & Chamberlain, 2006). Teachers emphasize that it's not simply the number of lines an actor has, but how well they're delivered that makes him/her worthy of an Oscar.

The success of the performance is measured by the acting skills of performers, including a convincing delivery of lines with voice, clarity, emotion, emphasis, and pacing—all the important facets of fluent reading. Rasinksi (2007) suggests that performing texts as in the performing arts is a highly authentic approach to fluency practice. And, it's easy and engaging.

Unlike typical theater, RT does not require memorization of lines, excessive props, or stages. It can be done in the classroom with minimal or no props. It stimulates imagination in actors and audience members to fill in the typical stage accoutrements with words, voice, movement, and gestures.

Actors read their lines from scripts throughout the production. After practice sessions, turn over the role of director to a student. Children relish that role and responsibility! Teachers have noticed a budding Cecil B. DeMille or two take the job quite seriously. When the director feels an actor needs to improve (e.g. on expression or voice tone), he cuts the action, models how the lines should be said, and restarts the scene. Recognizing fluency in others makes children consider their own and how to improve it (Clementi, 2010).

Flynn (2004) recommends practicing lines 15 to 20 times. This purposeful rereading brings notable improvement in all aspects of reading—a huge boost for struggling readers. When the script includes concepts related to curricular units of study, the rehearsal, review, and reactivation in RT practice improves children's assimilation of information and vocabulary (Clementi, 2010; Flynn, 2004). Practice can be done at home as well as at school.

Although teachers have done performances with some degree of spontaneity, there's a preparation protocol for readers' theater productions. Children must understand the steps taken beforehand and expectations for show time. See Figure 8.4 for the preparation protocol. Theatrical performances based on readings can take on the protocols of specific genres and venues.

RADIO READING

Nichols et al. (2009) describe a transformation of text that combines a readers' theater style of performance with audience improvisational discussion of the shared message. It's a combination of news broadcast followed by a lively conversation among news analysts; it's a highly motivating purpose for rereading as well as lively debate that deepens and expands comprehension while strengthening expressive language skills. The name for this activity comes from the image of a radio announcer talking to a listening audience. The procedure for radio reading is rather simple.

Schedule Readers' Theater as a weekly event just like any special area class. Children will know they can count on it happening; they'll look forward to the show. Invite special area teachers to help as part of fluency practice with students in their caseload. You can perform scripts as a class or have multiple shorter ones for different groups. Change it up from week to week. The content of scripts can relate to current units of study, providing review and solidifying children's learning of key concepts. Five days is just enough time to maintain interest and enthusiasm. Fridays are popular as the show date.

Day one: I introduce the material on the first day. Then, I read the book or script. We discuss the content, especially interesting dialog, information, or events. I reread the script with special emphasis on modeling appropriate fluency (e.g. expression, emphasis, and phrasing). Children reread the book or script with a partner.

Day two: Children work in teams on the class script or their group script. Individual parts aren't assigned at this point. Children read whatever part they've agreed to try or they read whatever part comes next in round robin fashion. In this way, everyone gets to try several parts. At the end of day two, roles are determined. Most of the time, children choose which part they'd like. When more than one person wants the same part, we draw straws or toss a coin to decide who gets it. Sometimes, I strategically assign parts to ensure individuals get practice where and when it's needed.

Day three and four: Practice, Practice, Practice! Children practice introducing the performance to an audience, introducing themselves and their part(s) (e.g. My name is ___ and I will be playing the part of ...), reading their lines, and adding gestures and movements. Small props and backdrops can be made at this time.

Make Stage Backdrops
Idea shared on teachers.net
Get an old white sheet or a piece of white material. On an overhead transparency, have kids draw a scene from the play as a backdrop. Attach the material to the ceiling and let it fall. Turn on the projector; place the drawing on the projector, centering the image on the sheet. You'll have an instant backdrop. Change the backdrop by changing the image on the projector.
   Work with one group while the other practices independently; then, switch. If you have permission from parents, videotape children during this practice. Watch the video as a whole class. Have children compliment fellow actors first; then, they can sensitively share a comment intended to improve the performance.

Day five: Performance! Invite other classes to the performance. Parents, administrators, teachers, and school staff are always welcome too.

Figure 8.4 Steps for Readers' Theater
Source Adapted from http://www.mandygregory.com/readers_theater.htm, retrieved March 27, 2010; Young and Rasinski, 2009, p. 8

First, a text appropriately suited for transformation into a journalistic structure is selected; it's also one that's at the group's instructional level. Then, the teacher reads it aloud with expression before the group rereads it chorally. The class collaborates on the genre transformation—changing the text from prose to a broadcast script. This reinforces children's ability to summarize and restate a message in another format. An assigned reporter is given time to practice her broadcast performance while others reread the text for content and prepare questions. When the reporter presents the news, others listen. When the broadcast is finished, the audience asks questions that stimulate conversation with the reporter; the teacher acts as mediator, relinquishing control to the discussants. Once one question is thoroughly explored, another is posed. In another session with this activity, a different student performs the broadcast (Tierney & Readence, 2000). See Figure 8.5. When done effectively, radio reading reinforces reading fluency, oral presentation skills, listening comprehension, the ability to summarize and restate information heard, and discourse skills.

Research consistently reports that, along with all of the benefits associated with repeated reading, reading for performing adds more—outcomes beyond what has already been noted. Performances based on repeated readings also increase engagement, motivation to read, and confidence (Clementi, 2010). For variety, teachers interject poetry study

Key Concepts

Genre transformation: changing text from one structure of writing (genre) to another.

Improvisation: creating an in-the-moment conversational response to a stimulus. In this case it would be the script read as a news account.

Discourse: discussion of a subject, debate, or conversation.

Discussants: those involved in a discussion or debate.

Poetry jam: session in which participants recite/perform poems by others or original work.

Transformation of prose to a radio broadcast script

The reporter broadcasts the news to an audience of listeners who ask follow-up
questions and discuss the content as news analysts

Figure 8.5 Radio Reading

followed by poetry performances as another venue; this allows continuance of fluency practice with a production that's new and different. Classes might schedule a *poetry jam* (performance of poetry) on Friday afternoons after everyone's had a chance to select a favorite poem for practice and dramatic reading.

POETRY JAM

Teachers in primary classrooms often use poems or verses from longer poems as text for shared reading. They put the text on a transparency and project it to a screen, creating a large text similar to a Big Book. Following the steps for shared reading, the poem is first read aloud. Then, there's conversation about its content. The children notice words and writing techniques; these are identified. Then, children are invited to reread the poem with the teacher; they do a *choral read*—together and out loud.

Wilfong (2008) suggests that poetry is ideal because it is "short text, [with] fun subject matter, and [an] easy match with the strategy of repeated reading" (p. 5). She offers steps similar to ones used for poetry jams.

A new poem is read aloud to the child to model how it should sound. It might be a favorite selected by the child or one the teacher chooses, considering children's reading levels and interests. Children can also perform poems for two voices. These poems have alternative lines for two readers or groups of readers who take the different parts—something like songs sung in a round. However, when reading the poems in two voices the individuals or groups don't overlap their reading as songs sung in a round overlap lyrics. You can use poems in books like *Joyful Noise: Poems for Two Voices* (Fleischman, 1988) or create your own by assigning lines from any poem to different readers. Readers perform some lines individually and other lines chorally in this approach, adding drama and emphasis. The activity is especially beneficial for small groups or partners at the same reading level.

The child rereads his poem with the teacher, a peer, an older student, a teaching assistant, a resource teacher, or a parent volunteer. Then, he practices the poem with any or many of these partners before taking the poem home to practice with someone. Just before the jam, each poet apprentice practices with a partner in the classroom.

As in RT, children can use minimal props—if they wish (i.e. sound effects)—to add interest for listeners (Faver, 2008; Wilfong, 2008). Children sometimes draw what they visualize from the words of the poem on a transparency; this could be projected onto the white sheet used as a backdrop for a readers' theater stage. Such personalization and drama never fail to make poetry jams events that are well remembered long after an academic year has finished.

Children keep a record of poems they performed. These are kept in a folder. They also like to keep a copy of the program handed out to the audience. It lists the performers for the day and the title of their selection. Children often like to try out a poem they heard someone else perform. They never fail to give their own twist to it! This activity builds reading proficiency *and* a love of poetry. Soon, children start to write and perform their own creations. Figure 8.6 lists websites with poems for reading and enjoying as well as guides for authoring certain forms of poetry.

Poetry jams bring "humor and pleasure in reading to struggling readers. [But] all students can benefit from fun texts and the intrinsic

http://www.poetry4kids.com

http://www.gigglepoetry.com/poetrytheater.aspx

http://ettcweb.lr.k12.nj.us/forms/newpoem.htm
Go to: Instant Poetry Forms and other links in the left column at this website.

Figure 8.6 Poetry Websites

rewards that result from confident, fluent reading" (Wilfong, 2008, p. 12). This activity does not require extensive or expensive materials; it's not time-consuming. It just needs time, patience, and the willingness to let children be creative (Faver, 2008). The activities described for varied repeated reading lead children to appreciate the qualities of a good performance; they recognize where work needs to be done.

> ## Key Concept
>
> **Songs sung in a round**: songs sung by splitting the singers into groups and having them start their part of the song at different times. Singers continue through the verses until the song is completed. Many camp songs are traditionally sung this way.

SELF-ANALYZING FOR FLUENCY

Working with a partner when practicing for readers' theater or a poetry jam, children easily recognize fluent reading that sounds just right. Teachers capitalize on this by having children assist with assessment. They use the Fluency Checklist for Student Partners (Figure 8.7) to report conclusions. Keep the terminology simple and the list short. The checklist is introduced in a mini lesson. The teacher reads aloud and children assess her performance. The class discusses that performance, including points of agreement and disagreement in scoring. This occurs over several days, making sure that all of the components of fluency are explicitly demonstrated at some point. Then, children practice with a partner and assess each other.

Not surprisingly, after evaluating someone else's fluency, children know just what to do to improve their performance. You sometimes

Place a check √ when your partner shows the behavior described below when reading.

Your partner:

_____ seemed confident about reading well

_____ read most of the words correctly

_____ read smoothly

_____ read word-by-word

_____ read some parts smoothly and other parts word-by-word

_____ read words in meaningful phrases

_____ used just enough expression in the right places

_____ repeated words or phrases when trying to self-correct or read for meaning

_____ repeated some words when trying to figure out an unknown word

_____ used the punctuation to make the reading sound right

Comments:

Figure 8.7 Fluency Checklist for Student Partners
Source Adapted from http://www.hslda.org/strugglinglearner, retrieved March 28, 2010

hear, "I did that (or I didn't do that). I should get a check there. I said it like this ..."

Fluency improves with instruction on its specific components and lots of time for targeted practice in meaningful activities. The teacher plans for both. But, individual improvements in fluency only become long lasting when the child understands the concept—what it is, why it's necessary, and how to achieve it. Self-assessment helps readers recognize and appreciate fluent reading.

Chapters 7 and 8 outlined ways to differentiate instruction to improve *text processing* (reading the words). Although children's skill in word reading accuracy and fluency limitedly indicates comprehension (e.g. through corrected miscues, appropriate expression), retelling allows teachers a much clearer assessment of the depth of children's understanding and connection building with text. Chapter 9 suggests ways to differentiate instruction to increase children's *meaning processing*—their comprehension of text read.

EXTENDING THE DISCUSSION

- Assess the fluency of readers in your classroom. Chart each. Discuss your findings with colleagues. How can you form groups? Plan instruction for the class's needs.
- Have students use the Fluency Checklist for Student Partners following instruction in fluency and modeling how to assess for each item. Share results with colleagues. How accurate were students? What did they learn? What modifications might be helpful?
- Plan for readers' theater in your classroom. Search for scripts with colleagues. Plan for performance dates.
- Plan a grade level poetry jam following a study of poetry and poetry writing. Use the websites listed or other resources.

9

DIFFERENTIATING INSTRUCTION
IN COMPREHENSION

MODELS OF COMPREHENSION

There has always been debate on the definition of comprehension (Fox & Alexander, 2009; Paris & Hamilton, 2009) and, more specifically, where a reader's understanding of the author's message resides (Bartine 1989, 1992). Some researchers theorize that meaning is constructed in the reader's mind *with* text rather than extracted *from* it (Smith, 1975); Rosenblatt (1978) proposed that comprehension is the result of a transaction between the reader and text. Despite differences in proposed definitions of comprehension, there seems to be agreement that understanding

> is affected by several groups of factors such as text (e.g. language structure, genre), reader (e.g. age, language and cognitive abilities, prior knowledge, metacognitive skills, motivation and interest), context (e.g. classroom literacy practices, teacher–student interactions), and task (e.g. test-taking, pleasure reading, retelling, sharing, scanning).
>
> (Paul & Wang, 2012, p. 37)

This consensus supports the need for differentiation as described in Chapter 1. The various stances on comprehension undergird strategies for gathering, organizing, and assimilating information from text, inferring, integrating, and accommodating meaning, and making connections within and beyond the text (Israel & Duffy, 2009; Ruddell

& Unrau, 2004); strategies that induce such behaviors are effectively taught when instruction is differentiated.

A plethora of comprehension strategies are easily discovered with a simple search of professional texts and journals (Block, Gambrell, & Pressley, 2002; Harvey & Goudvis, 2007; Tierney & Readence, 2000; Tompkins, 2003, 2010). These usually include varied combinations of text and meaning processing; they provide habits of mind that lead readers toward understanding. But, strategies used within and across texts need to be well matched to the different processes that competent readers conduct simultaneously (Irwin 2007; Routman, 2003; Tompkins, 2003, 2010). See Figure 9.1.

Teachers often confess that the strategy choices can become overwhelming. Readers wonder, "Which should I use?" For the most part, many strategies seem like different roads to the same destination.

Micro processes	Chunking words into meaningful phrases
Integrative processes	Building connections between sentences and paragraphs Understanding word referents Making mini inferences between sentences and paragraphs
Macro processes	Getting the gist—organizing and summarizing
Elaborative processes	Adding personally constructed meaning Creating mental images Responding affectively Making predictions Integrating prior knowledge Applying higher-level thinking
Metacognitive processes	Monitoring one's understanding Self-initiating fix-up strategies

Figure 9.1 Five Aspects of Comprehension
Source Tompkins, 2003, p. 205, 2010, p. 262; Irwin, 2007, pp. 2–7

Key Concept

Transaction (between reader and text): the reader and text continuously act upon and react to each other in unique ways. Each reader brings his history and prior knowledge to the active reading of a text, personalizing the interaction.

SEVEN KEYS FOR COMPREHENSION

Zimmermann and Hutchins (2003) have condensed this sea of ideas to *seven keys* [strategies] *for comprehension*. In this way, essentials are clear and the keys are comprehensive. The keys are outlined in this chapter. Although they're taught in a linear fashion—one at a time—for clarity, there's no hierarchical order to their use or importance. See Figure 9.2.

Proficient readers use these keys interactively. And, there's no single correct match of key to text. Readers choose the keys they need to construct meaning; often this will differ among readers. It's always interesting when children explain the strategies they used when and why. That's *metacognition* in action; children are thinking about their thinking (Irwin, 2007; Routman, 2003)!

Good readers use the strategies below to understand what they read; they use the right tool in the right place.

1. Create mental images or pictures in their mind

2. Use background knowledge called schema
They think about what they already know—from experience and/or previous reading on this topic.

3. Ask themselves thick and thin questions

4. Make inferences (the BIG "I")   ? ? ?
They read between the lines putting what's in the book with what's in their mind to conclude an idea called an *inference* (I).

$$I = tc + (e + bk)$$

5. Determine the main ideas (MI) or themes

6. Synthesize information
They combine the information from this text with what they know from experience and other texts. They check how and where it fits together.

7. Fix problems
They problem-solve hard words, errors, and confusions in meaning.

Figure 9.2 Keys for Comprehension
Source Zimmermann and Hutchins, 2003, pp. 5–6

The first key is *creating mental images*; this is also called *visualization*. Good readers create mental pictures of scenes and information in the text (Beers, 2003; Temple, Ogle, Crawford, & Freppon, 2011). These images include literal information from the text as well as inferred details based on one's background knowledge on the topic and personal experiences. As a reader advances to longer texts, "creating sensory images becomes even more critical in helping him remember and understand a more complicated story line" (Zimmerman & Hutchins, 2003, p. 33). The artistic liberty taken by readers when creating images is recognized in the movie version of any popular book. The producer's mental image can be very different from the picture a reader has visualized; readers infer details that elaborate and color their image—movie producers do too.

Another key is *integrating background knowledge*—including information and experiences. You already know how schema influences mental images. In addition, good readers think about what they already know related to the topic before they read. That activates thinking and expectations for what the author might tell. Vacca et al. (2007) report a strong relationship between background knowledge (schema) and comprehension; instructional levels "fluctuate from material to material depending on a child's schemata [plural for schema] and interest in the passage content" (p. 177). While reading, good readers consider whether the information in the text confirms what they know, adds to it, or contradicts it. If it contradicts their schema, they need to analyze which is correct—new or old information. This cognitive dissonance must be resolved before the new information can be assimilated and accommodated in the mind.

A third key involves *asking questions*. After surveying the text, efficient readers pose *thick* and *thin questions* they expect or hope will be answered by the author (Harvey & Goudvis, 2007; McLaughlin & Allen, 2000; Tierney & Readence, 2000). Thin questions focus on information found in the text—in one place or across several sentences and paragraphs. Thick questions require deep thinking about larger concepts associated with the content of the text. Answers to these questions are complex and *open-ended* (able to vary) because people mix personal sets of experience and schema with content in the text to construct them (Harvey & Goudvis, 2007). Readers search for and build answers as they read; their answers often generate more wondering. Such personal queries establish motivation for reading (McLaughlin & Allen, 2000). Manzo (1985) argued that readers who construct thick and thin questions throughout the reading act acquire an active inquiring attitude and the ability to consider alternative answers. See Figure 9.3.

The questions teachers ask become the kinds of questions readers ask themselves. Use the 5 Ws and 1 H to form all kinds of *thick* and *thin* questions (Harvey & Goudvis, 2007; McLaughlin & Allen, 2000).

Variations for each question word stem:

1. Who could...? Who should...? Who would...? Who might...? Who will...?
2. What could...? What should...? What would...? What might...? What will...?
3. When could...? When should...? When would...? When might...? When will...?
4. Where could...? Where should...? Where would...? Where might...? Where will...?
5. Why could...? Why should...? Why would...? Why might...? Why will...?
6. How could...? How should...? How would...? How might...? How will...?

Figure 9.3 Thick and Thin Questions
Source Harvey and Goudvis, 2007; McLaughlin and Allen, 2000

Next, active readers make inferences (I)—the *ah-hahs* in reading. Beers (2003) defines an inference as the "ability to connect what is in the text with what is in the mind to create an educated guess" (p. 62). Readers make *text-based inferences*—ones that can be supported with information explicitly stated in the text; they also make *knowledge-based inferences*—ones supported by their background knowledge and experiences as they connect to the content of the text (Beers, 2003). What's in the text (text content—tc) triggers thinking about experiences and background knowledge (e + bk). When tc combines with e + bk, voilà—an I is created. The formula is simple— I = tc + (e + bk)! That's the fourth key; it's referred to as *making inferences* or *reading between the lines*. It makes comprehension personal (Harvey & Goudvis, 2007; Irwin, 2007; Tierney & Readence, 2000). See Figure 9.4.

The fifth key is about deciding what's important. Proficient readers *decide on an overall main idea (MI) or theme* for the text when they've finished reading. There are different types of main ideas, including topic sentence, gist statement, or expression of a theme (Irwin, 2007). Readers' conclusions on any of these can vary to some degree and still legitimately connect to the text. Teachers need to clearly distinguish which type of main idea they are asking students to define; they should also ask readers to support the topic sentence, gist statement, or theme

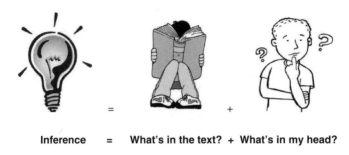

Inference = What's in the text? + What's in my head?

Figure 9.4 Making Inferences

they've identified. The reader recalls significant details in the text that support his conclusion; he also describes background knowledge and experiences that flavor his statements. Successful comprehension is demonstrated with an explanation of what the text was mostly about in one's own words rather than the reiteration of a topic sentence from the paragraph or passage (Zimmermann & Hutchins, 2003).

Good readers synthesize (combine) ideas from the text they're reading with what they know from experience and other reading (Block et al., 2002; Irwin, 2007). It's like adding ingredients to a funnel and having them form a mixture—something new and creative—as they come out of the bottom. Cain & Oakhill (2007) describe how synthesis works. In order to comprehend a text, the reader must initially integrate information from different sentences within the text; this establishes coherence across the passage. Simultaneously, the reader must incorporate background knowledge and ideas (retrieved from long-term memory) in order to make sense of details that might only be implicitly mentioned. This mental activity—*synthesis*—is the sixth key; it involves going *beyond the lines* of text.

Finally, proficient readers work to find and fix the problem whenever there's confusion (Block et al., 2002; Zimmermann & Hutchins, 2003). They are continuously acting metacognitively as they monitor their reading. Paul and Wang (2012) report that the National Reading Panel (2000) identified specific behaviors for effective comprehension monitoring. These include:

1) identifying where the difficulty arises, 2) identifying what the difficulty is, 3) reiterating via paraphrasing the difficult sentence or passage, 4) looking back through the text [to reread], and 5) looking

forward in the text for information that might assist in resolving the difficulty.

(p. 192)

These readers decide what tool to use and try it. If it doesn't work, they try another—and another. They persist until the problem is solved. *Fix-up work*, including self-monitoring and self-correcting, is the seventh key.

When readers apply the seven keys, they read with deep understanding. The keys provide a clear plan for decoding and comprehending. But readers need to know how and when to use each selectively and strategically.

Key Concepts

Cognitive dissonance: mental discomfort caused when competing ideas are held at the same time.

Topic sentence: a sentence in the text that expresses the central idea of a text.

Gist statement: a statement that conveys the essential information in a text.

THINKING OUT LOUD

Effective teachers introduce one key (strategy) at a time with a *think-aloud*—verbalizing thoughts as they read a book out loud (Beers, 2003; Irwin, 2007; Routman, 2003; Wilhelm, 2001). The process of thinking out loud makes the speaker's thought processes visible; they're ripe for reflection and analysis (Wilhelm, 2001). The behavior presents a model of how good readers actively engage with text, demystifying the thinking process required for successful comprehension. See Figure 9.5.

There's lots of demonstration, analysis of the teacher's strategy use, and discussion. Children practice applying and identifying strategies they've used in many situations with a variety of text types. The class continues until the keys are well learned—until children are *thinking along* as they read.

1. Tell children that you are going to say out loud what your brain is thinking as you read. It's going to sound a little unusual, but you want them to see how you figure out words and check understanding while you read along.
2. Explain that they should notice what you're doing and be ready to describe it when you finish reading.
3. Read the text aloud to children. Pause strategically to verbalize images, predictions, word-solving, self-corrections, and other strategies you're using. Emphasize a few strategies that are appropriate for the text. Don't overwhelm them with too much to notice.
4. After you finish reading, ask children to tell what kinds of things you did and the out loud thinking they heard.
5. Make a list, using their words to describe what they noticed. It might include things like

   • Made predictions

   • Problem-solved a hard word

   • Reread when it didn't make sense … etc.

6. Use this initial chart as a guide when you read another text. Ask children to watch for these or additional strategies. Emphasize some of the same as well as different strategies. Add new strategies to the list as children describe what you did this time.

   • Made pictures in your mind

   • Made inferences as you read

   • Asked questions and looked for answers … etc.

7. When the chart is complete, children will know how to think-along as they read. In post reading discussions, have children *download* their thinking by sharing which of the strategies on the chart they used to understand the text.

Figure 9.5 Doing Think-Alouds to Teach Readers How to Think-Along
Source Wilhelm, 2001, pp. 42–50

But, the teacher still does think-alouds now and then. Children also *download their thinking* in discussions, verbally explaining how they figured something out, came to a conclusion, or made an inference. The teacher asks, "What's your evidence?" Readers have to explain how they combined information in the reading with experience and background knowledge. The class analyzes how ideas vary based on the personal information different readers brought to the text. Such analysis leads children to consider new possibilities. When a key is well established—as a behavior readers can self-initiate—the teacher introduces another one.

Once children have acquired multiple useful tools (keys) on their reading toolbelt, they need to know how to select the right one for the job. The teacher guides readers toward specific keys at different points in the reading lesson. These soon become habits of mind as procedures for making sense whenever children read. See Figure 9.6. To assess successful integration of the keys for full and deep comprehension, teachers ask readers to retell.

Retellings indicate the degree of children's ability to self-initiate a clear, coherent expression of understanding as a literate response to reading text. The content of their retelling reflects success in applying the keys for comprehension. But, children need to understand what's expected in a retelling performance in order to do it well (Shea, 2000, 2006).

Before, During, and After reading, good readers are busy. They're using strategies for learning. They decide which tools to use for the text they're reading.

Before Reading

Before they read, good readers ....

- **look** at the title, cover of the book, and pictures inside.
- **think** about what they already know and what they want to find out.
- **predict** what the author will say or tell.

During Reading

While reading, good readers ....

- **tell** themselves what the author says.
- **make** pictures in their mind using what the author tells and what they know.
- **ask** themselves questions and look for answers.
- **identify** the main idea (MI) and important details.
- **predict** what will come next.

After Reading

After reading, good readers ....

- **retell** what they read and learned in their own words.
- **check** whether questions were answered.
- **plan** where they can find answers not found in the text.
- **decide** what was meaningful in the text and how well it was written.

Figure 9.6 When and How to Use the Keys to Comprehension

Key Concept

Habits of mind: ways of thinking that come naturally or automatically without conscious thought.

TEACHING RETELLING

Relevance is always the best place to start. Retelling is what we do as literate people when explaining experiences, conversations we've had, or texts we've read. When retelling, readers organize the understanding they've constructed from reading and report it to a listener. Brown & Cambourne (1987) describe retelling as "an all-purpose, extremely powerful learning activity ... providing 'on-task' practice of a range of literacy skills (reading, writing, listening, talking, thinking, interacting, comparing, matching, selecting, and organizing information, remembering, [and] comprehending" (p. 1).

And, retelling is more than a simple summary. It's a *summary plus*—infused with feelings, opinions, reactions, evaluations, inferences, and so much more. Competent readers don't wait for questions; their reporting is self-initiated and self-directed. The reader attempts to inform as well as influence an audience with literal information and personal interpretations (Shea, 2000, 2006).

Through their modeling, teachers let children observe exemplary retellings. The class discusses what the teacher told, how she made conclusions, and why she selected to share particular ideas. It's important to analyze the impact of the retelling on children's thinking. The teacher considers, "Did I convince them it's a good book? Are they excited about having the same experience with it?"

A thoroughly modeled retelling stimulates listeners' thinking. Children's responses in follow-up class conversations help teachers pinpoint areas to address in the next demonstration. It's essential to include demonstrations that are genre specific (e.g. narrative, expository) as well as format specific; readers can retell orally, in writing, or through drawing (Brown & Cambourne, 1987). Before expecting readers to effectively retell across different text structures and in different formats, provide exemplars for each variation.

MODELING RETELLING

The scoring procedure, previously discussed, is reviewed with small groups or individuals who are having difficulties. Examine the retelling checklists with the class, analyzing how items reflect the components of a successful retelling. Discuss how to score a retelling performance. As a child retells, areas he talks about are scored for *unassisted* retelling. He didn't need help or questioning.

If the speaker seems to have finished, someone asks, "Anything else?" Whatever the child adds at this point is still scored as *unassisted*. When the teller indicates he's finished, look at what has not been checked and form a question about that area. If he answers it, score it in the *assisted* column. The teller could talk about this information, but needed to be prompted or supported to do so; it wasn't self-initiated. Retelling scored as "assisted" as well as items with no score indicate areas for instruction. The teacher determines which key (strategy) needs to be taught, reviewed, and/or practiced; she plans how the intervention will be implemented.

Using an appropriate checklist, students evaluate and score the teacher's initial (unassisted) retelling with a partner. Then, children ask questions for areas missed and score the teacher's responses in the *assisted* column. Dyads form a group of four and compare scores they've given the teacher before sharing their results as a class. The children answer the teacher's queries, "What did I talk about? Where did I need assistance with questions?"

Scoring the teacher's retelling makes the process and assessment very clear. Ask for volunteers to take the teacher's place. Each volunteer models a retelling while peers score. Again, the class discusses these results. Now, everyone is ready to try retelling.

PRACTICING RETELLING

Children are assigned a partner. Partners read a text or listen to one read by the teacher. One child goes first; she retells while the listener scores the retelling checklist. Partners discuss the results while the teacher circulates to listen in and assist children as they work.

When each dyad has completed a retelling, get together to share results. The checklist scorers report their conclusions. Compliment each reteller before confirming scores and suggesting ways to improve performance.

In a subsequent practice session, roles reverse; the previous reteller listens while her partner retells. Practice and analyses continue with different partners until children feel comfortable and confident with the process and expectations. They should also be able to accurately articulate what was included and what was missing in each performance.

Form small groups for instruction when areas of need are similar. Some children need individualized reinforcement in many areas; others need intervention in specific ones. The teacher exaggerates any retelling component that presents a challenge to readers in her modeling; following the demonstration, her model is thoroughly analyzed with the child. Then, it's back to guided practice. The teacher observes and makes notes on the reader's progress. This debriefing with the reader encourages him to think about what he's doing well and where he needs to focus his attention.

SELF-ANALYZING RETELLING

Keep a record of retelling episodes with individual children. Score each and have the child score his retelling as well. Compare and discuss your results. What went well? What can be improved? Teachers find that children are amazingly accurate in this self-scoring. Dual scoring offers incredible insights, especially on the child's perception of his performance. In the after-reading debriefing (conference), discuss what would have been appropriate responses for areas on the checklist that the reader did not address on his own—or even with prompting.

At this point, children are prepared for retelling as a benchmark assessment of comprehension. A retelling for the teacher by a reader who fully understands the protocol of the assessment tool and is comfortable with the task provides valid data on his current level of performance(s); it also reliably identifies specific areas of need (Brown & Cambourne, 1987; Irwin, 2007; Shea 2000, 2006). After the retelling assessment, discuss scores with the child, pointing out success and goals for the next session. When assessment and evaluation become collaborative, learners contribute to goal setting. That leads to increased self-direction—to more metacognitive behavior. Children know what they know; and what they don't know, they plan how to find out. Proficient readers are those who have developed a wide range of self-sustaining skills—ones they can self-initiate when needed. At this level, children select and use strategies effectively, monitor comprehension, fix problems, and persist throughout a reading task. Each success increases their independence, confidence, and motivation.

Key Concept

Self-sustaining skills: skills that enable task success with relatively independent effort.

EXTENDING THE DISCUSSION

- Discuss the comprehension strategies taught in your school. Is there consistency? Would the seven keys model offer a better organization? Why? Why not? How could this be implemented schoolwide?
- Discuss the data and scores recorded on retelling checklists at the companion website.
- Share retelling checklists that you've completed with students in your class. Discuss what they show. How would you group children by needs? What would your first mini lessons be about?

10

CONCLUSION

PUTTING IT ALL TOGETHER

Each student presents a unique and interesting challenge to the teacher. The key word is *each*. In order to efficiently guide further learning, the student's acquired knowledge and skills must be accurately assessed. Although classrooms function as a collaborative community, they're composed of separate members with different interests, needs, abilities, and backgrounds.

Effective teachers remember to teach the individuals in any group. Differentiating instruction and interactions allow us to meet the academic, social, and emotional needs of students with the right amount of support and freedom.

ORGANIZING THE CLASSROOM

A good offense is the best defense. Classrooms with highly motivating, relevant curriculum, materials, and activities are places where learning problems are less likely to take hold. When they do, they are more quickly ameliorated; the key is well-informed responsiveness to learners' needs or readiness—at the onset. These classrooms are characterized by *authentic tasks*—ones connected to learning goals and outcomes and designed to meet students' interests, needs, or strengths. They are not simply assignments defined in programs with a one-size-for-all script. Authenticity is a cornerstone in any effective curricular design model. Day-to-day observation and assessment of students' performances on such tasks drive the planning for effective differentiated instruction and interventions. It's a continuous cycle of reflection and planning—teaching—observation and assessment—and back to the beginning; into the rhythm of this classroom routine, effective teachers are always mindful of elements that make a community thrive. See Figure 10.1.

"Careful attention to aspects for building settings that nurture learning, including field [environment], tenor [emotional tone], and mode [materials used] ensures that all children engage in literacy ... [activities] and flourish as language learners" (Shea, 2011, p. 44). Integrating sound theory and researched methodology, teachers teach differentially and children learn core concepts and skills in their own way, in their own time. They follow Smith's (1983) "one difficult [for the teacher] rule for making learning to read easy" (p. 23); that simple maxim suggests, "respond to what the child is trying to do" (p. 24). Effective teachers avoid curricular road maps defining rigid sequences and timelines—ones that inhibit responsive instruction. Instead, they interact with each child differentially to guide and support his next step in learning.

Resources for implementing such curriculum are multiple and varied, allowing teachers to accommodate the diversity found in any classroom.

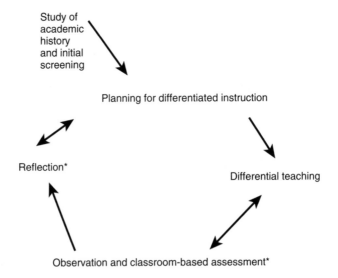

Study of academic history and initial screening

Planning for differentiated instruction

Reflection*

Differential teaching

Observation and classroom-based assessment*

*Areas with two-way arrows indicate where processes continue to inform practice both ways. Movement can be recursive at these points with in the cycle.

Figure 10.1 The Differentiated Teaching Cycle

However, the selection of appropriate resources must be done with intelligent eclecticism. Too often, this common-sense approach has been uncommonly applied in some schools; when that happens, the school becomes an institution of pedagogical inertia (Mayher, 1990).

Key Concept

Authentic learning task: an activity based as nearly as possible on real life experience where skills learned will be applied. The task requires learners to integrate skills, knowledge, and attitudes as they perform the task.

SOUND TEACHING SENSE

In the novel *Cutting for Stone*, Verghese (2009) defines an essential ingredient for success as a nurse. Using his words with an adjustment for teaching, one might argue that effective teachers seamlessly incorporate *sound teaching sense* to put all the elements discussed in this book—and other sources—together in a way that makes sense for each learner, for themselves, for their classroom, and for their school. "Sound [teaching] sense is more important than knowledge, though knowledge only enhances it. Sound [teaching] sense is a quality that cannot be defined, yet is invaluable when present and noticeable when absent" (p. 41). Teachers who have this quality have accumulated relevant research-tested knowledge and differentially, logically, and adaptively apply it. They are organized in the thinking and record keeping that informs actions.

MANAGING THE FLOW

Document, document, document becomes the mantra. Multiple forms of informal and formal assessment data are evaluated to conclude responsiveness or lack thereof to the instruction provided. RR reports are an essential part of this assessment–reflection–teaching cycle. They yield reliable data to inform responsive teaching, serving as "useful and productive lenses for what that is" (Mahyer, 1990, p. 286). Data of all types and forms as described in this text are systematically gathered, organized categorically, and reviewed with students, parents, and any grade-level, school, or RTI team.

INVOLVING ALL STAKEHOLDERS

The child as stakeholder needs to be involved at every step of learning. RRs, as discussed in this text, present opportunities for teacher–student collaboration. Learners are involved in self-assessment; they take ownership for improving performance.

Thinking together with the learner makes the analysis more accurate and the relationship stronger. An added bonus is that learners develop self-reflection skills that go far beyond what they do in the classroom.

Complete and copious notes, checklists, records, and work samples as artifacts support the teacher's reporting to RTI teams. The learner's portfolio provides authentic evidence for the conclusions reported when sharing the results of instruction with any of the stakeholders.

THE REWARDS

Implementation of any logical, reasoned instructional approach will only be effective when the tenets are understood, principles are adhered to with fidelity, and results are documented for detailed examination. Delivery protocols at all levels must be efficient, clear, and consistently applied.

In theory, differentiated instruction (and RTI) holds great promise. RRs as an assessment can inform planning for effectively differentiated literacy instruction. But, success is measured in details at the classroom level. Effective teachers use their knowledge and sound teaching sense to ensure that all children become literate.

BIBLIOGRAPHY

Allan, S. D. and Tomlinson, C. (2000). *Leadership for differentiating schools and classrooms.* Alexandria, VA: ASCD.

Allington, R. (1983). Fluency: The neglected reading goal. *The Reading Teacher,* 36, 555–561.

Allington, R. (2001). *What really matters for struggling readers.* New York, NY: Longman.

Altwerger, B., Jordan, N., & Shelton, N. R. (2007). *Rereading fluency: Process, practice, and policy.* Portsmouth, NH: Heinemann.

Anderson, K. M. (2007). Differentiating instruction to include all students. *Preventing School Failure,* 51(3), 49–54.

August, D. & Shanahan, T. (2006). *Developing literacy in second language learners: Report of the National Reading Panel on Language—Minority Children and Youth.* Mahwah, NJ: Erlbaum.

Ayers, W. (2001). *To teach: The journey of a teacher.* New York, NY: Teachers College Press.

Bartine, D. (1989). *Early English reading theory: Origins of current debate.* Columbia, SC: University of South Carolina Press.

Bartine, D. (1992). *Reading, criticism, and culture: Theory and teaching in the United States and England, 1820–1950.* Columbia, SC: University of South Carolina Press.

Beers, K. (2003). *When kids can't read: What teachers can do.* Portsmouth, NH: Heinemann.

Berk, L. E. & Winsler, A. (1995). *Scaffolding children's learning: Vygotsky and early childhood education.* Washington, DC: National Association for the Education of Young Children.

Bess, J. (1997). *Teaching well and liking it: Motivating faculty to teach effectively.* Baltimore, MD: The John Hopkins University Press.

Bissex, G. (1980). *GNYS at work: A child learns to read and write.* Cambridge, MA: Harvard University Press.

Block, C., Gambrell, L., & Pressley, M. (Eds.) (2002). *Improving comprehension instruction: Rethinking research, theory, and classroom practice.* San Francisco, CA: Jossey-Bass.

Boushey, G. & Moser, J. (2006). *The daily five.* Portland, ME: Stenhouse.

Boushey, G. & Moser, J. (2009). *The CAFÉ book.* Portland, ME: Stenhouse.

Brown, H. & Cambourne, B. (1987). *Read and retell.* Portsmouth, NH: Heinemann.

Brown, M. (1996). *Arthur writes a story.* Boston, MA: Little, Brown.

Bruinsma, R. (1980). Should lip movements and subvocalization during silent reading be directly remediated? *The Reading Teacher,* 34(3), 293–295.

Bunting, E. (2001). *Dandelions*. Orlando, FL: Harcourt, Inc.

Cain, K. & Oakhill, J. (Eds.). (2007). *Children's comprehension problems in oral and written language*. New York: Guilford Press.

Casey, S. & Chamberlain, R. (2006). Bringing reading alive through readers' theater. *Illinois Reading Council Journal*, 34(4), 17–25.

Cecil, N. (2007a). *Focus on fluency: A meaning-based approach*. Scottsdale, AZ: Holcomb Hathaway, Publishers.

Cecil, N. (2007b). *Striking a balance: Positive practices for early literacy*. Scottsdale, AZ: Holcomb Hathaway, Publishers.

Chard, D., Vaughn, S., & Tyler, B. (2002). A synthesis of research on effective interventions for building fluency with elementary students with learning disabilities. *Journal of Learning Disabilities*, 35, 386–406.

Clay, M. (1980). Early writing and reading: Reciprocal gains. In M. M. Clark and T. Glynn (Eds.), *Reading and writing for the child with difficulties* (Educational Review Occasional Publications no. 8), pp. 27–43, Birmingham, England.

Clay, M. (1987). *The early detection of reading difficulties* (3rd ed.). Portsmouth, NH: Heinemann.

Clay, M. (1990). *Reading: The patterning of complex behavior* (2nd ed.). Portsmouth, NH: Heinemann.

Clay, M. (1993a). *An observational survey of early literacy achievement*. Portsmouth, NH: Heinemann.

Clay, M. (1993b). *Reading recovery: A guidebook for teachers in training*. Portsmouth, NH: Heinemann.

Clay, M. (2001). *Change over time in children's literacy development*. Portsmouth, NH: Heinemann.

Clay, M. (2004). *Running records for classroom teachers*. Portsmouth, NH: Heinemann.

Clementi, L. B. (2010). Readers theater: A motivating method to improve reading fluency. *Phi Delta Kappan*, 91(5), 85–88.

Cole, A. (2004). *When reading begins*. Portsmouth, NH: Heinemann.

Cole, A. (2009). *Better answers: Written performance that looks good and sounds smart* (2nd ed.). Portland, ME: Stenhouse.

Collins, K. (2004). *Growing readers*. Portland, ME: Stenhouse.

Crawley, S. (2009). *Remediating reading difficulties* (6th ed.). New York, NY: McGraw-Hill Companies, Inc.

Cruickshank, D., Brainer, D., & Metcalf, K. (1999). *The act of teaching*. New York, NY: McGraw-Hill.

Cunningham, P. (2005). *Phonics they use: Words for reading and writing* (4th ed.). New York, NY: Pearson.

Daane, M. C., Campbell, J. R., Grigg, W. S., Goodman, M. J., & Oranje, A. (2005). Fourth-grade students read aloud: NAEP 2002 special study of oral reading. Washington, DC: U.S. Department of Education, Institute of Educational Sciences.

D'Angelo, K. (1979). *Silent rereading: Effect on reading speed and comprehension performance*. ERIC number 203291.

Davenport, M. R. & Lauritzen, C. (2002). Inviting reflection on reading through over the shoulder miscue analysis. *Language Arts*, 80 (2), 109–118.

Deno, S. L. (1987). Curriculum-based measurement. *Teaching Exceptional Children*, 20, 41–42.

dePaola, T. (1973). *Nana upstairs & nana downstairs*. New York, NY: Puffin Books.

Dixon-Kraus. L. A. (1996). *Vygotsky in the classroom: Mediated literacy instruction and assessment*. White Plains, NY: Longman.

Dodge, J. (2005). *Differentiation in action*. New York, NY: Scholastic.

Dolch, E. (1936). A basic sight vocabulary. *Elementary School Journal*, 36, 456–461.

Drame, E. & Xu, Y. (2008). Examining sociocultural factors in response to intervention models. *Childhood Education*, 85(1), 26–32.

Drapeau, P. (2004). *Differentiated instruction: Making it work*. New York, NY: Scholastic.

Earl, L. (2003). *Assessment as learning: Using classroom assessment to maximize student learning*. Thousand Oaks, CA: Corwin.

Eldredge, J. L. (2005). *Teaching decoding: How and why* (2nd ed.). Upper Saddle River, NJ: Merrill/Prentice Hall.

Fahey, J. (2000). Who wants to differentiate instruction? We did. *Educational Leadership*, 58(1), 70–72.

Faver, S. (2008). Repeated reading of poetry can enhance reading fluency. *The Reading Teacher*, 62(4), 350–352.

Fleischman, P. (1988). *Joyful noise: Poems for two voices*. New York, NY: The Trumpet Club.

Flurkey, A. (1998). *Reading as flow: A linguistic alternative to fluency*. Occasional Paper 26, Program in Language and Literacy, College of Education, University of Arizona.

Flurkey, A. (2001). How reading flows: An alternative to fluency. *Practically Primary*, 6(3), 29–33.

Flynn, R. (2004). Curriculum-based readers' theater: Setting the stage for reading and retention. *The Reading Teacher*, 58(4), 360–365.

Fountas, I. & Pinnell, G. (1996). *Guided reading*. Portsmouth, NH: Heinemann.

Fountas, I. & Pinnell, G. (2001). *Guided readers and writers: Grades 3–6*. Portsmouth, NH: Heinemann.

Fountas, I. & Pinnell, G. (2006). *Teaching for comprehension and fluency: Thinking, talking, and writing about reading*. Portsmouth, NH: Heinemann.

Fox, E. & Alexander, P. (2009). Text comprehension: A retrospective, perspective, and prospective. In S. Israel & G. Duffy (Eds.). *Handbook of reseach on reading comprehension*, pp. 227–239. New York: Routledge/Taylor & Francis.

Francis, D. J., Santi, K. L., Barr, C., Fletcher, J. M., Varisco, A., & Foorman, B. R. (2008). Form effects on the estimation of students' oral reading fluency using DIBELS. *Journal of School Psychology*, 46, 315–342.

Freeman, D. (1999). *Butterflies*. Cleveland, OH: Learning Horizons, Inc.

Fry, E. (1999). *1000 Instant words: The most common words for reading, writing, and spelling*. Westminster, CA: Teacher Created Resources, Inc.

Fuchs, D. & Fuchs, L. S. (2006). Introduction to response to intervention: What, why, and how valid is it? *Reading Research Quarterly*, 41(1), 93–99.

Fuchs, L. S., Deno, S. L., & Mirkin, P. K. (1984). The effects of frequent curriculum-based measurement and evaluation on student achievement, pedagogy, and student awareness of learning. *American Educational Research Journal*, 21, 449–460.

Gilbert, L. M., Williams, R. L., & McLaughlin, T. F. (1996). Use of assisted reading to increase correct reading rates and decrease error rates of students with learning disabilities. *Journal of Applied Behavioral Analysis*, 29, 255–257.

Goodman, Y. (1973). Psycholinguistic universals in the reading process. In *Psycholinguistics and reading*, ed. F. Smith, pp. 158–176. New York, NY: Holt, Rinehart, and Winston.

Goodman, Y. (1982). Miscues: Windows on the reading process. In *Language and literacy: The selected writings of Kenneth S. Goodman*, ed. F. Gollasch, pp. 93–101. Boston, MA: Routledge/Kegan Paul.

Goodman, Y. & Burke, C. (1972). *Reading miscue inventory: Procedures for diagnosis and evaluation*. New York, NY: Macmillan Publishing Company.

Goodman, Y. & Marek, A. (1996). *Retrospective miscue analysis: Revaluing readers and reading*. New York, NY: Richard C. Owen.

Greenwood, C., Tapia, Y., Abbott, M., & Walton, C. (2003). A building-based case study of evidence-based literacy practices: Implementation, reading behavior, and growth in reading fluency, K-4. *Journal of Special Education*, 372(2), 95–110.

Harvey, S. & Goudvis, A. (2007). *Strategies that work: Teaching comprehension for understanding and engagement* (2nd ed.). Portland, ME: Stenhouse.

Hasbrouck, J. & Tindal, G. A. (2006). Oral reading fluency norms: A valuable assessment tool for reading teachers. *The Reading Teacher*, 59(7), 636–644.

Hintze, J. M., Christ, T. J. & Methe, S. A. (2006), Curriculum-based assessment. *Psychology in the Schools*, 43, 45–56.

Hoyt, L. (2000). *Snapshots: Literacy minilessons up close*. Portsmouth, NH: Heinemann.

Hudson, R., Lane, H., & Pullen, P. (2005). Reading fluency assessment and instruction: What, why, and how? *The Reading Teacher*, 58(8): 702–714.

ILEA/Center for Language in Primary Education (London, England) (1989). *The Primary Language Record*. Portsmouth, NH: Heinemann.

Indiana Department of Education (2005). Academic standards and resources: *Fluency rubric*. Retrieved June 14, 2005 from http://www.indianastandardsresource.org/documents/1.pdf

Irwin, J. (2007). *Teaching reading comprehension processes*. New York, NY: Pearson, Allyn & Bacon.

Israel, S. & Duffy, G. (Eds.) (2009). *Handbook of research on reading comprehension*. New York: Routledge/Taylor & Francis.

Johns, J. (2008). *Basic reading inventory* (9th ed.). Columbus, OH: The McGraw-Hill Companies.

Kibby, M. (1989). Teaching sight vocabulary with and without context before silent reading: A field test of the focus of attention hypothesis. *Journal of Reading Behavior*, 21(3), 261–278.

Klingel, C. & Noyed, R. (2001). *Mouth* (leveled reader). New York, NY: Rosen Publishing.

Kuhn, M. & Stahl, S. (2000). *Fluency: A review of developmental and remedial practices*. CIERA Rep. 2–008. Ann Arbor, MI: Center for the Improvement of Early Reading Achievement.

Kusuma-Powell, O. & Powell, W. (2004). January 17–18. *Differentiation: Operationalizing inclusion*. Paper presented at EARCOS Weekend Workshop, International School of Kuala Lumpur, Kuala Lumpur, Malaysia.

Leslie, L. & Caldwell, J. (2011). *Qualitative reading inventory* (5th ed.). New York, NY: Allyn & Bacon.

Levin, E. (1993). *If you traveled on the underground railroad*. New York, NY: Scholastic.

Littky, D. (2004). *The big picture: Education is everyone's business*. Alexandria, VA: ASCD.

Manzo, A. V. (1985). Expansion models for ReQuest, CAT, GRP, and REAP reading/study procedures. *Journal of Reading*, 28, 498–503.

Mayher, J. (1990). *Uncommon sense: Theoretical practice in language education*. Portsmouth, NH: Heinemann.

McKenna, M. C. & Stahl, S. A. (2003). *Assessment for reading instruction*. New York, NY: Guilford Press.

McLaughlin, M. & Allen, M. B. (2000). *Guided comprehension: A teaching model for grades 3–8*. Newark, DE: International Reading Association.

Millis, K. & King, A. (2001). Rereading strategically: The influence of comprehension ability and a prior reading on the memory of expository text. *Reading Psychology*, 22(1), 41–65.

Morrow, L. (2007). *Developing literacy in pre-school*. New York, NY: The Guildford Press.

Murray, R., Shea, M., & Shea, B. (2004). Avoiding the one-size-fits-all curriculum: Textsets, inquiry, and differentiated instruction. *Childhood Education*, 81(1), 33–35.

National Reading Panel (NRP) (2000). *Report of the National Reading Panel: Teaching children to read*. Washington, DC: Department of Education.

National Research Council. Reading development checklist. In *Report on Preventing Reading Difficulties*. Retrieved August 17, 2011 from http://www.readingsuccesslab.com/Reading_Development_Checklist.htm

Neumann, V., Ross, D., & Slaboch, A. (2008). *Increasing reading comprehension of elementary students through fluency-based interventions*. M.A. Action Research Project, Saint Xavier University and Pearson Achievement Solutions, Chicago, IL, ERIC number ED 500847.

Nichols, W. D., Rupley, W. H., & Rasinski, T. (2009). Fluency in learning to read for meaning: Going beyond repeated readings. *Literacy Research and Instruction*, 48(1), 1–13.

O'Connor, J. (2008). *Fancy Nancy sees stars*. New York, NY: HarperCollins Publishers.

Oglan, G. (2003). *Write, right, rite!* New York, NY: Allyn & Bacon.

Ohanian, S. (1999). *One size fits few: The folly of educational standards*. Portsmouth, NH: Heinemann.

Ohlhausen, M. M. & Jepsen, M. (1992). Lessons from Goldilocks: "Somebody's been choosing my books but I can make my own choices now!" *The New Advocate*, 5, 31–46.

Paris, S. & Hamilton, E. (2009). The development of children's reading comprehension. In S. Israel & G. Duffy (Eds.). *Handbook of research on reading comprehension*, pp. 32–53. New York: Routledge/Taylor & Francis.

Paul, A. (1992). *Shadows*. New York, NY: Scholastic.

Paul, P. & Wang, Y. (2012). *Literate thought: Understanding comprehension and literacy*. Sudbury, MA: Jones & Bartlett Learning.

Pettig, K. (2000). On the road to differentiated practice. *Educational Leadership*, 58(1), 14–18.

Pinnell, G. S. & Fountas, I. C. (1998). *Word matters: Teaching phonics and spelling in the reading/writing classroom*. Portsmouth, NH: Heinemann.

Pinnell, G. S., Pikulski, J., Wixon, K., Cambell, J., Gough, P., & Beatty, A. (1995). *Listening to children read aloud: Oral fluency*. Washington, DC: National Center for Education Statistics, U.S. Department of Education. Retrieved July 14, 2005, from http://nces.ed.gov/pubs/web/95762.asp

Prior, S., Fenwick, K., Saunders, K., Ouellette, R., O'Quinn, C., & Harvey, S. (2011). Comprehension after oral and silent reading: Does grade level matter? *Literacy Research and Instruction*, 53, 183–194.

Raffi, (1987). *Down by the bay*. New York, NY: Random House.

Rasinski, T. (2000). Speed does matter in reading. *The Reading Teacher*, 54(2), 146–151.

Rasinski, T. (2003). *The fluent reader*. New York, NY: Scholastic.

Rasinski, T. (2006). Reading fluency instruction: Moving beyond accuracy, automaticity, and prosody. *The Reading Teacher*, 59(7), 704–706.

Rasinski, T. (2007). Teaching fluency artfully. In R. Fink & S. J. Samuels (Eds.), *Inspiring reading success: Interest and motivation in an age of high-stakes testing*, pp. 117–140. Newark, DE: International Reading Association.

Rasinski, T. (2008). *Evidence-based instruction in reading: A professional development guide to fluency*. Boston, MA: Allyn & Bacon.

Rasinski, T. & Hoffman, T. (2003). Theory and research into practice: Oral reading in the school literacy curriculum. *Reading Research Quarterly*, 38, 510–522.

Reutzel, D., Jones, C., Fawson, P., & Smith, J. (2008). Scaffolded silent reading: A complement to guided repeated oral reading that works! *The Reading Teacher*, 62(3), 194–207.

Rock, M., Gregg, M., Ellis, E., & Gable, R. A. (2008). REACH: A framework for differentiating classroom instruction. *Preventing School Failure*, 52(2), 31–47.

Rosenblatt, L. (1978). *The reader, the text, and the poem*. Carbondale, IL: Southern Illinois University Press.

Routman, R. (2003). *Reading essentials: The specifics you need to teach reading well*. Portsmouth, NH: Heinemann.

Ruddell, R. & Unrau, N. (Eds.). (2004). *Theoretical models and processes of reading* (5th ed.). Newark, DE: International Reading Association.

Ryan, C. (2009). *Monkey to the top* (level F benchmark book). Tuscon, AZ: Reading A-Z, Learning Page, Inc.

Samuels, S. J. (1979). The method of repeated readings (reprinted 1997). *The Reading Teacher*, 50(5), 376–381.

Samuels, S. J. (2002). Reading fluency: It's development and assessment. In A. E. Farstrup & S. J. Samuels (Eds.), What research has to say about reading instruction (3rd ed.), pp. 166–183. Newark, DE: International Reading Association.

Scanlon, D., Anderson, K., & Sweeney, J. (2010). *Early intervention for reading difficulties: The interactive strategies approach*. New York, NY: Guilford Publications, Inc.

Schreiber, P. (1980). On the acquisition of fluency. *Journal of Reading Behavior*, 12(3): 177–186.

Schumm, J., Vaughn, S., & Leavell, A. (1994). Planning pyramid: A framework for planning for diverse student needs during content area instruction. *The Reading Teacher*, 47, 608–615.

Scott, R. (1993). *Spelling: Sharing the secrets*. Toronto, Canada: Gage Educational Publishing Company.

Shaw, C. (1988). *It looked like spilt milk*. New York, NY: HarperCollins.

Shea, M. (2000). *Taking running records*, New York, NY: Scholastic.

Shea, M. (2006). *Where's the glitch?: How to use running records with older readers, grades 5–8*. Portsmouth, NH: Heinemann.

Shea, M. (2011). *Parallel learning of reading and writing in early childhood*. New York, NY: Routledge/Taylor & Francis.

Shea, M., Murray, R., & Harlin, R. (2005). *Drowning in data?: How to collect, organize, and document student performance.* Portsmouth, NH: Heinemann.

Silver, H. F., Strong, R. W., & Perini, M. J. (2001). *Tools for promoting active, in-depth learning.* Trenton, NJ: Thoughtful Education Press.

Smith, F. (1975). *Comprehension and learning: A conceptual framework for teachers.* New York, NY: Richard C. Owens Publishers, Inc.

Smith, F. (1983). *Essays into literacy.* Portsmouth, NH: Heinemann.

Sousa, D. A. (2001). *How the brain learns.* Thousand Oaks, CA: Corwin Press.

Stecker, P. M., Fuchs, L. S., & Fuchs, D. (2005). Using curriculum-based measurement to increase student achievement: Review of research. *Psychology in the School, 42,* 795–819.

Stecker, S., Roser, N., & Martinez, M. (1998). Understanding oral reading fluency. In *Forty-seventh yearbook of the National Reading Conference,* T. Shanahan and F. V. Rodriguez-Brown (Eds.), pp. 295–310. Chicago, IL: National Reading Conference.

Stiggins, R. (2002). Assessment crisis: The absence of assessment *for* learning. *Phi Delta Kappan, 83,* 758–69.

Temple, C., Ogle, D., Crawford, A., & Freppon, P. (2011). *All children can read: Teaching for literacy in today's diverse classrooms* (3rd ed.). New York, NY: Pearson.

Therrien, W. & Kubina, R. (2007). The importance of context in repeated reading. *Reading Improvement,* 44(4), 179–188.

Tierney, R. & Readence, J. (2000). *Reading strategies and practices: A compendium* (5th ed.). Boston, MA: Allyn & Bacon.

Tobin, R. (2008). Conundrums in the differentiated classroom. *Reading Improvement,* 45(4), 159–169.

Tomlinson, C. (1995). *Differentiating instruction for mixed-ability classrooms.* Alexandria, VA: ASCD.

Tomlinson, C. (1999). *The differentiated classroom: Responding to the needs of all learners.* Alexandria, VA: ASCD.

Tomlinson, C. (2000). Reconcilable differences? Standard-based teaching and differentiation. *Education Leadership* 58(1), 6–11.

Tomlinson, C. (2001). *How to differentiate instruction in mixed-ability classrooms* (2nd ed.). Alexandria, VA: ASCD.

Tomlinson, C. (2004). Differentiation in diverse settings. *The School Administrator,* 61(7), 28.

Tomlinson, C. (2008). The goals of differentiation. *Educational Leadership,* 66(3), 26–30.

Tomlinson, C. & Strickland, C. (2005). *Differentiation in practice: A resource guide for differentiating curriculum, grades 9–12.* Alexandria, VA, ASCD.

Tompkins, G. (2003). *Literacy for the 21st Century: A balanced approach* (3rd ed.). Upper Saddle River, NJ: Merrill Prentice Hall.

Tompkins, G. (2010). *Literacy for the 21st century: A balanced approach* (5th ed.). New York, NY: Allyn & Bacon.

Topping, K. (2006). Paired repeated reading: Impact of a tutoring method on reading accuracy, comprehension, and fluency. In T. Rasinski, C. Blanchowicz, & K. Lems (Eds.), *Fluency instruction: Researched-based best practices,* pp. 173– 191. New York, NY: Guilford Press.

Vacca, J., Vacca, R., Gove, M., Burkey, L., Lenhart, L., & McKeon, C. (2003). *Reading and learning to read* (5th ed.). New York, NY: Allyn & Bacon.

Vacca, J., Vacca, R., Gove, M., Burkey, L., Lenhart, L., & McKeon, C. (2007). *Reading and learning to read* (7th ed.). New York, NY: Allyn & Bacon.

VanDerHeyden, A. M., Witt, J., & Gilbertson, D. (2007). A multi-year evaluation of the effects of a response to intervention (RTI) model on the identification of children for special education. *Journal of School Psychology*, 45, 225–256.

Vaughn, S., Mathes, P., Linan-Thompson, S., Cirino, P., Carlson, C., & Pollard-Durodola, S. (2006). Effectiveness of an English intervention for first grade English language learners at-risk for reading problems. *The Elementary School Journal*, 107(2), 153–180.

Verghese, A. (2009). *Cutting for stone*. New York, NY: Vintage Books, Division of Random House.

Vygotsky, L. S. (1978). *Mind and society: The development of higher mental processes.* Cambridge, MA: Harvard University Press. (Original work published in 1930, 1933, and 1935.)

Whitmore, K., Martens, P., Goodman, Y., & Owocki, G. (2005). Remembering critical lessons in early literacy research: A transactional approach. *Language Arts*, 82(5), 296–307.

Wilfong, L. (2008). Building fluency, word-recognition ability, and confidence in struggling readers: The poetry academy. *The Reading Teacher*, 62(1), 4–13.

Wilhelm, J. D. (2001). *Improving comprehension with think-aloud strategies*. New York, NY: Scholastic.

Yatvin, J. (2004). *A room with a different view: How to serve all children as different learners.* Portsmouth, NH: Heinemann.

Young, C. & Rasinski, T. V. (2009). Implementing readers theatre as an approach to classroom fluency instruction. *The Reading Teacher*, 63(1), 4–13.

Zimmermann, S. & Hutchins, C. (2003). *7 Keys to comprehension: How to help your kids read it and get it!* New York, NY: Three Rivers Press.

INDEX